Outsourcing Security

Outsourcing Security

A Guide for Contracting Services

JOHN D. STEES

BUTTERWORTH
HEINEMANN

Boston   Oxford   Johannesburg   Melbourne   New Delhi   Singapore

Butterworth–Heinemann supports the efforts of American Forests
and the Global ReLeaf program in its campaign for the betterment
of trees, forests, and our environment.

Library of Congress Cataloging-in-Publication Data
Stees, John D.
    Outsourcing security : a guide for contracting services / John D.
Stees.
        p.   cm.
    Includes bibliographical references and index.
    ISBN 0-7506-7023-1 (alk. paper)
    1. Private security services—United States.   2. Police, Private—
United States.   3. Police—Contracting out—United States.
4. Contracting out—United States.   I. Title.
HV8291.U6S74   1998
363.28'9—DC21   98-21893
                                                      CIP

British Library Cataloguing-in-Publication Data
A catalogue record for this book is available from the British Library.

The publisher offers special discounts on bulk orders of this book.
For information, please contact:

Manager of Special Sales
Butterworth–Heinemann
225 Wildwood Avenue
Woburn, MA 01801-2041
Tel: 781-904-2500
Fax: 781-904-2620

For information on all Butterworth–Heinemann publications available,
contact our World Wide Web home page at: http://www.bh.com

10 9 8 7 6 5 4 3 2 1

Printed in the United States of America

Contents

Acknowledgments

I have read somewhere that no person can write a book alone. Because this wise saying is especially applicable in this instance, I wish to thank those countless men and women in the security community who have taught me something new each day of my career. My added thanks are extended to the many security contractors who have instructed me in some of the inner workings of their businesses and to those who became good friends as well as business associates, especially to a good friend Alex Trent, who has graciously made a significant contribution of information for this book. My very special appreciation goes to Joanne Roth, Patricia Huber, and Janet Schaeffer. Their years of constant professional dedication, loyalty, and support are beyond measure. Without their confidence, this book would not have been written.

Introduction

Outsourcing Security Services has been written for the purpose of assisting security managers, consultants, proprietors, contract administrators, purchasing officers, and other management officials who may become involved in the complex decision-making processes associated with the selection, procurement, and monitoring of contract security officer services and other security-related responsibilities. This material is also applicable to organizations that use those services but feel the need to reevaluate the productivity and cost effectiveness of their current contractor. Managers of contract security officer companies may find new ideas and strategies within these pages that may enhance their marketing and proposal preparation efforts and provide new insights for improving management quality and customer satisfaction.

The expense of security services, whether provided by a contractor or hired directly by the user company, often represents one of the largest cost burdens an organization might experience within its security or loss prevention budget. This cost must be thoughtfully balanced against the value of assets the security officer service is employed to safeguard and the value of other collateral services the security officers might provide. In recent years, many companies have become more aware of those costs and have redirected their focus toward reducing security expenses. One of the many cost-saving initiatives the industry has implemented is replacement of proprietary security officer employees with contract services. Unless a user organization takes a systematic approach when selecting and negotiating with a contract service and monitoring postaward activity, the savings often can be an illusion.

In the writing of this book, an assiduous effort has been made to offer proved managerial processes that follow a logical sequence and that management may use as an effective guide to ensure that the use of value-added protective services is appropriately balanced against the cost of quality performance. It is a reference work that provides practical suggestions for resolving the many questions and pitfalls encountered in the design and development of security organizations. Special emphasis is placed on utilization of contract security service providers.

Within these pages, some readers may perceive some similarities between a few of the strategies being recommended and a management way of life known as total quality management. This is not entirely unintentional. TQM means different things to different people, and companies often adopt their own interpretations of the concept to suit their specific requirements and operations. Regardless of how TQM is applied, it can be broadly viewed as a process in which an organization finds that it must thoroughly depart from old paradigms and engage in constant states of improvement that exceed those of their competitors in terms of speed, cost, quality, productivity, and satisfaction. The ultimate goal is a condition in which the organization has refined and perfected each of its operations to the degree at which it can assume the role of being a premier leader in its field.

In addition to using strategies such as TQM or any of its variations to achieve this goal, companies throughout the country are placing increased reliance on third parties to provide quality goods and services. Contracting security services can be a perplexing problem, because it involves in-depth planning, management, training, plan administration and implementation, systems design, policy development, and myriad other elements essential to the establishment of a total and effective program that will bring value to the client. It is intended that this book assist the reader in resolving concerns regarding outsourcing security services and aid the reader in achieving a healthy and satisfactory relationship with the contractor.

The first chapter is a brief overview of the evolution of contract security services in the United States from the nineteenth through the twentieth centuries. The remaining chapters are devoted to topics more directly associated with the considerations of outsourcing. These involve the beneficial use of teams for security planning purposes, the selection, procurement, and monitoring of contract security services, the selection and use of investigation firms, obtaining security services in foreign countries, and providing suggestions for achieving value-added services from contractor-provided security functions.

Outsourcing Security Services attempts to eliminate many of the obstacles to quality performance of a contract and dispels some of the misperceptions associated with the discipline of contract security service. The book is intended as an aid to business managers and executives to make reasonable and prudent decisions regarding the type and extent of security services best suited to the unique requirements of their organizations. When it is deemed appropriate to use a contract security service provider, this book offers methods by which management can chart a course to the successful and cost-effective achievement of that goal.

1

A Century of Change

One might rightfully question the relevance between a historical glimpse at the private security profession and the concept of outsourcing. The purpose is to describe the integral role of the private security industry during its years as a structured and at times unstructured profession. The legacy of some historic events resulted in consequences within the business that have greatly influenced the manner in which security services, particularly contract services, are being performed and perceived today. This chapter is not intended to be all inclusive, because this subject has been addressed in one form or another by many historians more knowledgeable of the development of this unique vocation. Some of their writings, including some older documents written by participants or witnesses to some of the events described herein, have provided a wide source of factual reference for this material.

The background of the private security industry is reviewed merely to show that the outsourcing of private security firms has a history and momentum of its own and is not a recent development of our changing times. By having a comprehension of the conditions that aided the expansion of private security firms and some of the events that over time influenced the contracting of services, the reader may better understand how the past of the private security business affects the present.

IN THE BEGINNING

The history of security is as old as that of humanity. The instinctive need for self preservation, protecting one's life and property, was as much a concern to the primitive cave dwellers as it has been to all of their successors through the intervening millennia. As civilizations and nations developed with increasing populations, the people inhabiting them relied heavily on the force of government and feudal armies for protection. Although a medieval king's army might protect a country from foreign invaders, it did almost nothing for people living in remote farms, villages, and towns who wanted only to live an orderly life and to safeguard their property from fellow humans who could not understand why they should not be allowed to use animal strength and cunning to get what they wanted. A solution evolved by which the people would employ other private individuals to protect them. This action may have been the seed of the private security organization that when planted would take many centuries to produce a fruitful harvest.

EARLY LAW ENFORCEMENT AND PRIVATE SECURITY

In the United States, the slow growth of public law enforcement in the formative years was an important factor in the development of private security organizations. Historically, police responsibility was left to the local communities, which were virtually independent from one another. Although large eastern cities possessed a semblance of law and order in the form of city marshals, public watchmen, and constables, formally organized police departments did not begin to appear until the nineteenth century. Many of these were inept, inadequate, corrupt, or politically manipulated and were usually held in low esteem by the citizens. These departments lacked the personnel and resources necessary to cope with the extent of crime that preyed on the burgeoning businesses and industries that were suddenly erupting on the American scene.

The local police were impeded by the fact that they had no jurisdiction beyond the boundaries of the political entity they represented. With the exception of the Texas Rangers, formed in 1835, there was a general dearth of law enforcement agencies under the direct control of a state or the federal government until the formation of the U.S. Secret Service in 1860. The lack of extra jurisdictional authority and general incompetence of local police and the absence of state or federal police organizations were among the substantial influences that produced a void in the protection of lives and property and that would ultimately be filled by private security firms.

As with any other embryonic discipline, a certain vocabulary emerged in the early years in which many different names and titles of security organizations were synonymous. The terms *private police, private detective, independent police, secret service, detective police,* and similar designations were usually interchangeable according to the audience the user wished to impress. The generic term *security* did not appear until later years, when the use of the word *police* was limited by law for use only by individuals or agencies commissioned with law enforcement authority. In some states, *security* may now include industrial or special police authorized with powers of arrest granted under state or municipal laws. During most of the 1800s, the private security industry was generally unregulated and was able to use broad discretionary interpretations regarding the use of titles and particularly the power of arrest by citizens, which these security forces were. They considered themselves substitutes for inadequate police departments, and in most cases, they assumed their authority as being the same as public police officers—a condition that would eventually change.

THE EARLY YEARS OF PRIVATE SECURITY

In his book, *The Pinkertons,* James Horan expressed the belief that the earliest private guard agency in the United States was established in Boston in 1821 and was employed by merchants in that city when the city watchmen failed to apprehend criminals committing burglaries. Another private independent police agency opened in New York in 1845, followed by another in St. Louis, Missouri, in 1846, with similar organizations being established in Baltimore, Philadelphia, and Chicago during the same period. These private agencies known as *specials* were in general competition with the local police, whose competency was still questionable. No laws restricted the purpose of the specials and much of their authority was self-assumed. In the early 1850s, a Scottish immigrant named Alan Pinkerton established a private detective agency that would begin a dynasty and thrust the private security service industry into the next millennium. Other organizations of this nature would soon follow because the time and opportunity were ripe.

Momentous events were occurring during these years that would have a profound effect on the social, political, and economic future of the country. As early as 1838, military expeditions were forging west to plot new routes for the settlers who were soon to come. Western outposts were being created for trading purposes and as a place for westbound travelers to rest. The California Gold Rush hastened the momentum as thousands of families poured across the plains to look for instant wealth or at least opportunity. Trade and gold were not the only reasons for westward expansion. Eastern politicians were determined to take Manifest Destiny to its limit and extend the boundaries of the country to the Pacific Ocean. They, too, saw remarkable opportunities for wealth. America was getting richer, a fact that did not escape the bold and creative minds of those with criminal intent. There were opportunities for everyone.

THE RAILROADS AND THE LAND OF DETECTIVES

The 3,000 miles that separated the east coast from the west in the early nineteenth century was an impediment to the accelerating pace of the country's expansion. Freight and passengers travelling by wagon train and stage coach required arduous weeks of travel and a great deal of good fortune to reach their destinations. Mail service by Pony Express lasted only 16 months and resulted in financial failure to its owners. The requirement for rapid, dependable transportation was the problem, and the railroads had the answer.

Railroads had laced the eastern seaboard since the 1830s, and by 1857 they were advancing toward the west. On May 10, 1869, a historic event occurred at Promontory Summit, Utah. It was there that the rail lines of the Central Pacific and Union Pacific railroads were joined to form a line that connected Sacramento, California, to Omaha, Nebraska, and established the first continental railroad.

Within the next 20 years, four more transcontinental railroads were operating through service to the Pacific states. For the first time, the country was linked by rail, and the golden age of the railroad had begun. It could also be said that it began the bronze age of private security.

The assets of express companies and railroads were exposed to all types of crime. Warehouses and boxcars were broken into and pilfered, terminals were destroyed, passengers on trains were robbed, expressmen were killed, vandals tore rails from the roadbed to derail locomotives, and internal theft was rampant. The companies were completely vulnerable to these and other offenses. Because the trains traveled through various states, jurisdictional restraints and the absence of federal or state authority made recourse to local police a futile effort. Western expansion of express companies and railroads only compounded an immense problem. In many areas of the new territories, law enforcement was still nonexistent. These conditions created an opportunity for private security firms to fulfill a critical need as railways and express companies sought outside help that could transcend geographic boundaries to pursue criminals and safeguard assets.

What may have been the first major contract for protecting private property was awarded in 1855 to Alan Pinkerton by a coalition of eight midwestern railroads to protect their interests and assets. This landmark agreement, together with other notable contracts with express companies, propelled Pinkerton's already thriving business into a position of national prominence and acclaim. Such recognition would also bring the budding private security industry to the attention of big business and aid in its expansion throughout the eastern and midwestern states. Again, according to James Horan, "the proliferation of these organizations was so significant in the Chicago area that it was said that the State of Illinois was known as the 'land of detectives.'"

DIVERSIFICATION FROM HONESTY ASSURANCE TO GUARD FORCES

Most of the work of the private security forces during the early years was devoted largely to investigations of criminal offenses and "spying" on employees to ensure their honesty. Although covert investigations and spying on employees were tactics anathema to the Victorian culture of the times, it was an accepted practice by railroad management to maintain control of far-flung conductors, station masters, and other hirelings, as it was with other businesses. It was also a tactic that would bring the private security industry under considerable scrutiny and criticism in years to come.

Although detection provided an important source of income for private security firms, uniformed guard services were beginning to make a substantial contribution to the steady revenue of agencies that offered them. Public distrust and the inadequacies of the local police to protect the property of the growing number of commercial businesses created a demand for protection that the private security sector fulfilled by providing uniformed guards, often as a supplement to the detection services. The use of uniformed security personnel preceded the use of uniforms by city police officers by many years and was viewed with mixed opinion. Many city police departments preferred that their officers wear plain clothes. They shunned uniforms because they were symbolic of militarism, a concept that was not welcomed in a democratic society. It was not until the middle of the nineteenth century that the officers of police departments were finally put into uniforms, some of which closely resembled those worn by private guards. At times, the distinction between the two services was not immediately apparent, but the events of the succeeding years would have a profound effect on the evolution of the private security profession and determine its eventual destiny.

PRIVATE SECURITY AND MILITARY INTELLIGENCE

The years immediately before, during, and after the Civil War added another dimension to the private security industry. Again it was Alan Pinkerton who achieved most of the notoriety, but not as much as he thought he deserved. Although the use of spies was prevalent by both sides, neither the Union nor the Confederacy possessed the advantage of a structured intelligence apparatus until the middle years of the war. The gathering of military information was an ad hoc and erratic process in which ordinary citizens were pressed into the business of espionage, which was poorly planned and nebulous in purpose. Although Pinkerton had no military experience, he recognized the need for spying as a mechanism to gather vital military information and volunteered his services to the Union.

Through an association with Major General George McClellan, Pinkerton was hired to operate a "secret service" for the government in 1861, but the position lasted only as long as McClellan remained in favor with President Lincoln, which was not long. Although Pinkerton claimed credit for many exploits, including the arrest and imprisonment of the infamous Rose Greenhow, a Confederate spy operating in Washington, and tracking down enemy agents and southern sympathizers, his further exploits in gathering military information were less than remarkable and frequently unreliable.

The role of being the Chief of Secret Service was not to be Pinkerton's sole province, because Lieutenant General Winfield Scott had hired another man, Lafayette Baker, to run a parallel secret service. There was no cooperation between Baker and Pinkerton, and their agents often arrested one another. The animus between Pinkerton and Baker and the political atmosphere that prevailed in 1862 caused Pinkerton to resign from the field of military espionage in protest of conniving politicians and return to more familiar ground. Perhaps Pinkerton's greatest distinction during this period was that he is deemed the first private contractor to provide security-related services for the United States government.

THE BALTIMORE PLOT

The most widely known event for which Pinkerton received recognition as a military spy was the discovery of an alleged murder plot against President-elect Lincoln. According to Pinkertons' records, he was in possession of information that indicated the assassination was to occur in Baltimore as Lincoln and his entourage traveled through the city en route from Harrisburg to Washington. Pinkerton arranged an elaborate plan by which Lincoln would travel surreptitiously through Baltimore on the North Central Railroad and arrive safely in the nation's capital.

This escapade would eventually become a highly disputed issue that may never be resolved. In an account of the alleged conspiracy to assassinate Lincoln on his journey to Washington, Ward H. Lamon, a close friend of Lincoln and a participant in Pinkerton's plan, described his later belief that the plot was "mere fiction." This belief was fortified in a book, *Baltimore and the Nineteenth of April,* written by George W. Brown, mayor of Baltimore in 1861 and later chief justice of the Baltimore Supreme Bench. Brown asserts that there was no such plot and that Pinkerton "was carried away by [his] own frightened imagination." Whether there was such a conspiracy will never be known, but Lamon records that "Mr. Lincoln soon learned to regret his midnight ride."

PRIVATE SECURITY AND THE LABOR MOVEMENT

Industrial growth and western expansion during the post–Civil War period breathed new life into the private security profession as more business organizations employed contractors to protect their property. This was particularly evident as the nation moved into lawless areas of the far west and as megaindustries were being developed in the east. Another factor that stimulated the expansion of the private security industry was the growing disputes between management and labor organizations.

Private security firms provided agents who covertly infiltrated labor unions and reported their activities to management. These agencies also supplied private police forces that were used extensively by railroads, mining interests, and other corporate entities to control or dispel striking workers and to protect corporate assets, often with disastrous results. Strikes were frequently accompanied by murder, violence, and destruction of property and at times required intervention by the few state militias that then existed or by the army when private police were unable to control a situation. Blame for violence and unethical or illegal behavior passed vehemently between the unions and the private security industry. The allegations of illegal activity by private security organizations involved in strikes enraged the unions and provoking sympathy for organized labor among certain members of congress.

THE HOMESTEAD INCIDENT

The animosity between labor organizations and the private security industry erupted on July 4, 1892, at the small Pennsylvania town of Homestead, the home of the Carnegie, Phipps Steel Company, which was in the throes of a strike. The company had hired Pinkerton to move on the strikers and to protect the property. Early in the morning several hundred guards from three states sailed by barge to Homestead and were fired on by the strikers when they arrived. The guards returned fire, and a 12-hour siege ended when the guards surrendered. When the smoke cleared and the dead were counted, 13 people had been killed. This historic event contributed heavily to end of the generally unfettered ability of private security agencies to freely engage in interstate activity and the exercise of police powers by private citizens. It was no longer to be business as usual.

CONGRESSIONAL INVESTIGATION OF PRIVATE SECURITY

The deadly confrontation at Homestead and other violent clashes between private guard forces and strikers elsewhere, but almost simultaneously with that event, became the catalyst that caused Congress to initiate a federal investigation of the private security industry in 1893. Heated and emotion-filled rhetoric, testimony, and intense debate flowed back and forth during the proceedings. The entire private security industry was portrayed as agents provocateur and evil mercenaries, which are anathema to a constitutional form of government. It was also claimed that the private security industry had infringed on the authority of government to preserve public order and to maintain the peace and tranquillity of the people.

The defense focused on the dismal failure of the states and the federal government to provide adequate protection to businesses that served the purpose of free enterprise. It further directed the committee's attention to the need for private security organizations that would effectively fill that void. The congressional investigating committee agreed. In a report titled *Investigations in Relation to the Employment for Private Purposes of Armed Bodies of Men or Detectives in Connection with Differences Between Workmen and Employers,* the committee stipulated that any effort to regulate the private security business should come from the states and should not be within the province of the federal government.

Through the months of testimony given in this investigation, the public was finally made aware of the extent to which the private security industry had become a part of the American scene. The states reacted quickly to the recommendations of these hearings. Within seven years, 24 states and the District of Columbia passed legislation that prohibited armed private guards from other states from entering their jurisdictions. Additional laws were passed that strictly regulated the powers of arrest of guards employed by private security agencies. In many states, these restrictions are in force today.

THE TWENTIETH CENTURY

At the turn of the twentieth century, private security companies were still heavily involved in strike breaking and labor disputes, and they continued to spy on union activity for the next 40 years. Other agencies gradually shifted away from this volatile business as the public began to view labor with a different and more sympathetic perspective. These agencies were attempting to put the aftermath of Homestead behind them and dispel the hostility and distrust it engendered in the minds of the working class.

Private guard and watchmen services were flourishing as industry and commerce rapidly expanded and diversified. The luster of their tarnished public image was being restored as they were increasingly being contracted to patrol retail businesses, jewelry stores, banks, race tracks, and other businesses, because the nature of private security was still perceived as being more dependable than that of the public police. Alliances were being formed between the security industry and various trade associations that increased the recognition of the industry as a contributing part of the business community. During the following decades, private security companies mushroomed throughout the cities of the United States. Most of these concentrated solely on providing detection services as Americans were becoming more aware of the extent of criminality that accompanied Prohibition and the Great Depression. The growth of the private security industry during the preceding 100 years was largely influenced by the ineffectiveness of local public law enforcement and the absence of state or federal police forces.

PUBLIC POLICE REFORMS

The increasing awareness of the U.S. public about the issue of rising crime and gang rule caused citizens to expect more from civil authorities. Reforms slowly began that would place public law enforcement in competition with the private police. Although many police departments remained politicized, the use of technology, education, and modern techniques began to make inroads into the field of crime detection and the eventual professionalization of urban police organizations. The time had come for many of the services provided by private security organizations for more than 100 years to be accomplished by governmental law enforcement agencies. The use of in-house security organizations began in earnest as early as the 1900s. As the private security industry became more regulated and restricted in its interstate activities, private industries began to hire their own security organizations. One interesting reason was to cut the increasing costs of private security operations, quite the opposite of the current philosophies of outsourcing. Over time, the use of in-house guard services became more popular, especially in organizations that employed former military and police officers in managerial security positions. These persons brought with them a philosophy wherein they were more comfortable having control of their own guard forces than relinquishing most of that direction to an outside organization. They found certain relationships and interdependencies that existed between other elements of the company.

To these companies, the expense of a proprietary security force was justified by the perceived benefits. Some large governmental and defense contractor firms employed in-house security officer forces because at least part of the costs for these organizations often was reimbursed as part of the general and administrative expenses funded under federal contracts. These charges were eventually challenged by the government, which asserted that contractor security-officer companies could perform equivalent services at less cost.

Because of these challenges, surveys and studies comparing proprietary with contracted security services were conducted by industry and organizations such as the Aerospace Industries Association and the American Society for Industrial Security. The conclusions were generally the same: private security organizations could do the job less expensively that proprietary forces. Other companies were becoming more aware of the costs of a proprietary security force and were making their own decisions regarding the matter. They, too, began considering whether there was value in changing to a contract service.

The changeover was not immediate. There was no sudden rush to convert a long-standing proprietary security force to one supplied by contractors. Even though the expense of an in-house security force was evident, many executives believed it was better to stay with the devil you knew rather than to go with an unknown devil. However, other events were occurring that would help modify existing concepts. The private security industry itself was changing to meet new demands. Traditional management styles were making the transition to new ways of doing business through implementation of total quality management concepts and similar strategies focused on continuous improvement.

Security firms that formerly provided traditional services began to be acquired by organizations that had diverse interests and disciplines. An adjustment had to be made in which security services would be integrated into new and different fields, many of which required a new understanding of technology, management, marketing, and communication. It became quite evident that to remain competitive, the private security industry had to improve their capabilities to offer a full range of services that would reach into areas not previously envisioned. To fail in the objective might mean disaster, but to succeed, the leaders in the industry recognized the fact that they must focus on the quality of their expanded services and the value potential they would bring to a user organization.

In recent years, the winds of change have been whipped to gale force, given impetus by industry's focus on global competition. In the final analysis, the objectives are to be more productive and to reduce costs. From a security standpoint, companies that may have been slow to examine the costs of productivity of their proprietary security forces began putting that function under close and exacting scrutiny. A trend began among a number of businesses to outsource security services to private contractors. Others made the determination that for a variety of valid reasons, it would be in their best interest to retain an in-house security service. Although many support functions are being outsourced to third-party vendors, one of the most widely contracted services continues to be security officer operations and other functions associated with the security organization. This would include such services as investigations, consultations, armored car services, and executive protection. It has already been estimated that more than one half of all organizations employing security officer services have depended on those provided by contractors. Many companies throughout the United States have begun making the transition from proprietary forces to contract providers as a means of containing costs. Whether this trend can be considered an experimental exercise or whether it will gain momentum depends on contractors' ability to provide the level of quality service required by an organization at an acceptable cost.

PRIVATE SECURITY MEETS NEW CHALLENGES

The great leaps of modern technology within the past 20 years, such as biometric identification and digital closed-circuit television, compounded by the stimulus of competition provided many choices and challenges to the private security industry. Traditional activities, such as guard and investigative services, continued to supply a substantial source of revenue, but progressive companies found the need to diversify into more technical and sophisticated lines of business to meet the changing demands of their customers.

The resurgence of international terrorism and the concern for ensuring the safety of Americans living and working in foreign environments and providing domestic executive protection services added another dimension to the challenges of the private security industry. As governmental agencies began to privatize many services, the contract security industry responded by providing fire-fighting teams and equipment, medical and rescue personnel, prisoner transportation, marine patrols, security administration, and a plethora of similar activities.

It is also interesting that some of the services provided by private security contractors included the provision of armed law enforcement officers authorized with the power of arrest at some large government complexes and the use of paramilitary special weapons and tactics teams at sensitive installations. These new disciplines required special skills, training, and investment unknown to the private security business decades before. Many of the radical changes brought about by the diversification of business also produced remarkable changes in management structure and philosophies. The colorful, bearded, and ultraconservative private security managers and employees who rode on horseback in the past gave way to staffs of well-educated professional people and chief executives with outstanding business and management acumen. Today the private security industry is a major international business with an employee base that vastly exceeds that of all U.S. law enforcement agencies and with technical resources that would rival those of many police departments.

SUMMARY

The private security industry began by providing an essential service to the United States at a crucial time in its history. The expansion of the industry paralleled the expansion of the nation as it spread from coast to coast. Its growth was largely the result of the early function it served as an alternative to the absence of efficient police forces and jurisdiction because of those fearful of expanding governmental power. Regardless of the occasional scandal and suspicions that would ultimately affect any unregulated and generally unrestrained business, there was hardly a period in which private security enterprises did not progress. Even war and economic depression failed to impede their continued development; in some cases, they added to it.

In many respects, the private security industry laid the groundwork for the techniques and administration of many modern law enforcement agencies and created technologies and scientific solutions to problems unique to the security and law enforcement professions. For more than 150 years, the U.S. private security industry has constantly changed its initiatives and resources to satisfy the demands of its customers, and is doing so today. Businesses now in the throes of reorganizational revolution are depending heavily on the private sector to provide protective services that may have previously been obtained through proprietary sources. The final results rest in the processes used to determine the type of service best suited to users' requirements and selection of the most effective contractor to fulfill those needs.

2

Internal Teams

This chapter is a discussion of some of the practical means a business may consider for creating a preliminary design for an efficient and cost-effective security function within a company. It is further intended to aid management in defining the type of protective service most appropriate for their overall requirements. The method being proposed is use of a security project team that begins by envisioning the type and scope of a security program harmonious with the needs and culture of an organization. It then follows the process through a variety of stages of study and research to reach an objective conclusion and assist in determining which services may be best served through outsourcing.

This chapter discusses the role of teamwork in regard to the issue of outsourcing and gives reasons why the use of third-party contractors has become a growing concept within U.S. industries. Reasons are shown why the value of decisions made by a multidisciplined team transcends that of decisions made by a single entity and how such a team may be formed and function as a viable tool in designing a security program that is reasonable and prudent for the organization it serves.

WHY OUTSOURCE?

Outsourcing became the growth industry of the 1990s. Its popularity stemmed from organizations' burgeoning recognition that if an activity is not a core competency and does not allow them to differentiate their companies from others, they should consider contracting the function to an outside expert. In earlier years, if a company turned over business processes to an outsider, it was often considered to be a sign of internal difficulty or instability. This is not true today, since the acceleration of outsourcing services indicates that it has become the rule rather than the exception. It is now considered to be a mainfestation of business acumen.

In 1996, The Outsourcing Institute estimated that $100 billion was spent on outsourcing and projected that outsourcing among U.S. organizations, companies of all sizes and government at all levels, would grow by more than 35% during the following year. It anticipated that areas likely to show the greatest increases are human resources, logistics, information technology, and support services. This would include security-related functions, because these responsibilities are often managed from within the human resources or support services activities.

The decision to retain proprietary security functions or to outsource them requires much introspection, research, and study. This would involve an assessment of the entire spectrum of the company operations and its culture. It would necessarily include the security requirements of the company and the services provided by a security organization and the customers it serves. When, what, how, and to whom such services are to be outsourced contributes to the complexity of that challenge. Making such decisions requires labor-intensive and time-consuming efforts that constrain time-poor executives from performing effectively. Realizing this, an executive may refer the matter to internal teams, which frees the executive to spend more time on strategic initiatives critical to the company's success.

In deliberating whether to outsource a security function, the team should keep in mind the Top Ten Reasons to Outsource, which are as follows:

1. To improve company focus
2. To gain access to world-class capabilities
3. To accelerate benefits of reengineering
4. To share risks
5. To free resources for other purposes
6. To reduce or control operating costs
7. To make capital funds available
8. To make cash infusion
9. Resources are not available internally
10. The function is difficult to manage or out of control

Source: The Outsourcing Institute, 1996.

It is not expected that each of these reasons to outsource will always be entirely applicable to the various projects the team may undertake, but they provide a good frame of reference for the team to consider in future actions.

TEAMWORK VERSUS SINGLE-ENTITY DECISIONS

For the purposes of this book, a security project team is defined as a number of persons associated in a joint action. Some members may be project specific, and their work has a short lifespan. Other members may be engaged in ongoing security-related undertakings. If, for example, it is suggested that a security force is the most appropriate choice for a company, the security project team can choose whether it should be a proprietary force or one provided by a contractor.

This can be a complex task that requires the contribution of thoughts and recommendations from diverse groups of people working within the organization. There are myriad influences to be considered, including issues such as staffing, training, legal and liability ramifications, financial resources, regulatory standards, managerial philosophies, vulnerability and criticality factors, use of technology, and an endless list of other elements that must be kept in mind when making such a decision. These considerations emphasize the fact that except in rare instances, the design of a security organization is a responsibility that should not be undertaken by a single entity.

As larger companies focus more on centralization of the security function, many local security managers of multifacility organizations may feel they have less influence on corporate decisions being made at a home office. For example, when a determination is made to outsource security service, the entire process of soliciting bids, preparing specifications, writing a request for proposal, conducting contract negotiations, and selecting a supplier often falls within the purview and discretion of a purchasing or procurement officer or another official at the corporate level who has similar responsibilities or influence. There are instances in which these activities are performed by an entity whose focus is directed solely at the bottom line cost of the service without any serious consideration of the practical safeguarding requirements of the organization. Without being informed of such requirements, the procurement officials frequently have no intimate acquaintance or comprehension of the total security requirements of the company.

This problem can usually be avoided when there is bilateral communication between the procurement official and each operating element of the company. This same premise would be applicable whether operations are in distant locations or all in one building. In the absence of specific knowledge of operational requirements, the procurement official may have no recourse but to proceed in good faith to accomplish the task of selecting a security service on the basis of simple standards. The selection may be determined by the procurer's personal perceptions and interpretations of the type of service a provider is expected to furnish, but it may not fulfill the security requirements of the organization. If the operational elements do not make their security requirements known before the procurement process begins, the results can be less than anticipated. The need for continuing reciprocal communication between the security project team and the procurement official is essential to ensure that quality services are provided.

CONSEQUENCES OF UNILATERAL DECISION MAKING: A CASE STUDY

The following case study demonstrates some of the consequences of failing to establish bilateral communication regarding security requirements. This situation involved a large defense contractor with multiple divisions and branch offices throughout the United States. Some of these organizations had employed proprietary guard services whereas others used a variety of contract guard services procured at the local level. Several of the divisions were performing work on sensitive government contracts that required the guard personnel to possess government-granted security clearances. The personnel security clearances were necessary because the facilities depended on the guard services to provide the supplemental controls necessary to protect classified material in accordance with prevailing government regulations. Local conditions also dictated that the guards be licensed to carry sidearms, be certified in emergency response training, and have special technical training to monitor and operate sophisticated electronic intrusion detection and access control systems. Organizations that used contract guard services had developed successful long-term alliances with their providers and enjoyed the teamwork that resulted in many security-related commendations and awards from their government customers.

A corporate decision was made to replace all proprietary guard forces and various guard contractors with one national guard service provider as a cost-containment measure. This initiative was dictated by the corporate procurement office, which proceeded without recognizing the unique operational security concerns of the different facilities involved.

The specific security requirements of the local organizations consequently were not included in the statement of work submitted to the bidders, and the successful contractor was unaware of them until the transition date arrived. It was learned that the replacement guards possessed neither the required personnel security clearances nor any of the required training certifications and licenses necessary to work at the facilities. It was also determined that the local field offices of the contractor lacked the capabilities to obtain government security clearances and were unprepared and unfunded to provide the necessary training and licensing of guard personnel. This matter was exacerbated by the fact that in the absence of this essential information, the contractor's bidding price and salary range were so low that none of the incumbent guards who had the qualifications could be retained. The capability of these facilities to safeguard classified information and to protect valuable assets was severely impaired and jeopardized the facilities' ability to perform on government classified contracts unless emergency security measures were taken to mitigate the adverse effects of the decision. The expenses incurred by divisions to ameliorate these effects and restore their adherence to contractual security obligations exceeded the cost-savings expectations of the corporate office. The further consequences of presumptively directing the employment of a contractor on the basis of the sole premise of the lowest price also resulted in use of an inferior service and produced a long-term degradation of security performance.

Unfortunately, this example is not unique. It is only one of others that exemplify the consequences of an uninformed entity mandating unilateral decisions that may have a profound effect on the course of a total organization.

CONSIDERATIONS FOR TEAM STRATEGIES

As a substitute for having a single entity make decisions regarding security matters, a number of enterprises have taken more positive and practical approaches for envisioning a comprehensive security program. These businesses have discovered that by using the team concept they might identify and resolve complex issues in a manner that defines new and innovative actions that lead to a desired result. In the 1990s businesses of all sizes used teams to study and develop innovative strategies to assist their organizations in becoming more competitive. These enterprises broke down the old bureaucratic barriers that separated different functions and created a new organizational environment in which people can cooperate. They discovered the value-added benefit of teamwork by instilling a shared sense of being a part of the business and energizing a mutually interdependent group. This same concept may be applied to the establishment of a security project team that uses a holistic philosophy to determine the safeguarding requirements of a business.

The team concept is particularly useful as companies begin to envision the scope of asset-protection services needed for the organization and the position in which security works as a part of the management structure. Teams should be cross functional, because the security organization provides a service to all elements of a company, each with its own requirements and expectations regarding the manner in which assets are to be protected and the type of protective organization to safeguard them. Each team member brings a variety of perceptions regarding his or her concerns and those of the constituencies represented. Through discussion and analysis of these perceptions, common objectives emerge that can be used as a preliminary blueprint for the final design of the security system.

These teams must have the absolute support of top management from the very beginning if they are to succeed. When there is only nominal support, it may be because management is unprepared to make the required commitment when the project is to be turned into reality, particularly if the team recommends transition from a proprietary security function to one provided by a contractor. Experience has shown that decisions to make a transition with a security service are frequently met with substantial resistance because they involve all of the adverse considerations associated with layoffs. The need for top management support is necessary to preempt such resistance and provide the momentum that allows the initiative to reach fruition. One method to help ensure managerial support is publication of a written policy directive by the highest executive within the business sector that officially forms the team. The policy further identifies the purpose of the team and the responsibilities of the members and bestows its authority to function. The policy approach helps awaken the slumbering interests of managers who might otherwise be less than enthusiastic about the security function and stimulate their support and participation.

QUALIFICATIONS OF TEAM MEMBERS

The qualifications of the team members participating in a security project team are critical to its success. They must be goal-oriented persons with the focus, motivation, and enthusiasm to push the project to completion. They also should have a broad perspective regarding the overall mission and culture of the company and its customers. The members should be analytical and creative and possess tact and good communication skills. They should have a propensity for organizational development and problem solving. As with any other team, members must be cooperative and supportive of each other in working toward a common set of goals. Every company has employees with these qualities who can be brought together to develop a sense of working principles, clarify objectives, and foster a sense of cohesion and unity. Teams such as these allow the participants to develop a sense of commitment to the project and buy into the initiatives of the company, which directs the manner in which its assets are to be protected. By having such commitment, the team assumes control of the project, which creates accountability for its success.

DEVELOPING THE TEAM

Any team must have a strong sense of focus and measurable goals. An early objective of a security project team is to establish an overview of the security functions of the company as they relate to the business purposes and core competencies of the organization. Achieving this objective aids the team in envisioning improved value-added concepts that can be implemented.

The team must have rules of engagement that encourage a strong sense of purpose and direction. These include election or appointment of a leader or facilitator to maintain team momentum and establish agendas; a time-keeper who controls the amount of time established for resolving specific issues; and a scribe to record all proceedings to avoid note taking by individual members. These duties may be rotated from one meeting to another to ensure that all members have an opportunity to participate equally and share in the responsibilities of design.

When a security organization currently exists within a company, the security manager should be a critical participant in the team. The security manager may be the only person in the company who has intimate knowledge of the security function, its structure, and the different challenges it must confront. These challenges vary according to the peculiarities of the company's operations and include issues such as compliance with applicable government security regulations and adhering to health, safety, and environmental standards. These are but a few of the many considerations with which the security project team has to become familiar. Any team effort to improve the security function must give primary emphasis to meeting these requirements and any other state or local regulations that direct their activities.

The security manager may provide historical information to the team and be able to identify strengths and weaknesses and help define vulnerabilities an inexperienced person may not immediately recognize. These issues present an area of consideration if a decision is made to outsource any of the security responsibilities or modify existing agreements the company may have with a contractor providing security services.

PREPARING THE TEAM

Before any action is undertaken by the team, there must be an educational period in which the team is indoctrinated in fundamental security concepts. Security often has been described as a state of mind, and because team members normally are representatives of different constituencies, they have their own perceptions and thoughts regarding the level of security they deem appropriate for the entire company. These perceptions also are influenced by the personal security awareness and life experiences of the individual team members. For example, employees who reside in high-crime areas and must walk through a dimly lit parking lot at the close of a midnight work shift to go to their cars may have a different view of a need for security than those who live in relatively crime-free areas and leave work during daylight hours. This same concept is applicable to the professional concerns of each team member. The concerns of a facilities maintenance manager may focus on protection of the physical plant, whereas an information systems manager has more interest in computer security.

Making the distinction between the existence of an actual problem within a company and employees' perception that a problem exists challenges the ability of the team to understand how people think and their capability to separate the existence of a problem from the perception of one. The team should be sufficiently perceptive to differentiate an imaginary problem from one that can actually be corrected. One method to resolve this conflict is to compare both the stated problem and the person's expectations of a particular issue. As a rule, when an individual's expectation is equal to his or her perception, the problem is a valid one. When there is a wide disparity between expectations and perceptions, the problem may be a perceived one and may not actually exist.

It is necessary to educate team members to the point at which they have a general understanding of the purpose and functions of the security organization and a familiarity with interests of the other team members. It is not intended that every team member become a security professional. It is intended that a state of mind be achieved wherein each team member understands the basic concepts and mission of the security organization before the team can identify and resolve problems. In many businesses, this might involve a study of similar companies to determine what they are doing successfully. Although this approach has merit, every business has unique qualities, concerns, and vulnerabilities related to geographic location, physical layout, operational activities, past security incidents, and myriad other influences that affect the level of security reasonable and prudent to protect their assets. The techniques and strategies that appear to work well in one company may not be entirely applicable in another. It is important to consider that security is a condition in which one size does not fit all. Any study of another company's security program used as a model should be viewed in the full context in which it is structured and the threats and vulnerabilities it is designed to neutralize or prevent.

Familiarizing the team in basic security philosophies normally is a task assigned to the security manager or the person responsible for administering the asset protection programs of the company. Companies without this resource may be at a disadvantage without this knowledge and it could impede the productive actions of the team. At the minimum, it would make their task more difficult. One option available to the team to resolve this matter is selection of an independent professional security consultant to provide insights and guidance.

GETTING THE TEAM STARTED

Once formed, the security project team must be committed to follow the task to completion to assure continuity of purpose. This includes commitment of time, energy, effort, active participation, cooperation, open communication, and intellectual resources. Assuming that participation in the security project team is an adjunct to their usual work routines, team members should be prepared to arrange their schedules to allow attendance at the meetings and to assume additional tasks, such as studies, research, report preparation, or other assignments that may be relevant to achieving the team's objectives.

All team participants must be willing to engage in open dialogue in which they can share their thoughts and opinions on the matters being discussed. On many teams, there are a few who remain reticent and are reluctant to contribute their ideas or suggestions regardless how meaningful they might be. Others attempt to control the discussions and insist that their philosophies are the only correct ones. Although both types of behavior may appear to be deleterious to the efficient working of a team, both participants might also have valuable contributions to make if encouraged to present them in a cooperative manner. If such encouragement is not fruitful, consideration should be given to replacement of these team members.

The team members should be receptive to new ideas—even dramatic and radical suggestions should not be dismissed without consideration. Team members also must be prepared to confront distasteful options. For example, outsourcing a function often involves replacing or transferring long-term company employees. If alternative employment cannot be found within the company, these employees are subject to layoff or forced retirement. Making such a decision is difficult and disturbing, but the team must be ready to accept accountability if the recommendations are implemented. It might be good to review the experiences of a company that has overcome some of the difficulties mentioned earlier.

THE ARBITRON STORY: A CASE STUDY

Progressive companies are finding remarkable success in the use of teams to enhance security operations and processes. One example is the Arbitron Company. Arbitron is a leading provider of broadcast audience estimates and provides a broad range of media research and information services.

Early security programs were administered under the traditional "command and control," position and power paradigm. Policies and procedures were developed in an introspective manner by beleaguered experts in the function assigned to life safety programs. Some policies and procedures were perceived by the workforce as sending stone tablets down from on high. There was no conversation or explanation regarding the relevance to the employee or the company or why employees would be under the threat of progressive discipline, up to discharge, if they violated certain policies. In this respect, the employees became victims of the system, a condition that would be challenged by the empowered workforce of today.

In 1993 conditions existed that forced Arbitron to exit from a segment of its marketplace, and a large portion of the workforce was reduced as a result. This difficult and traumatic event enabled the company to leap forward on the evolutionary path. A totally new organization was in development and positioned to respond quickly to a rapidly changing marketplace. It was obvious that the traditional paradigms were not working and that the era of command and control was over.

New focus was provided by executive management that restructured the organization and inverted the pyramid. In this type of management structure, information flowed down to the executive team, and being equipped with this new perspective, the team supported the organization, rather than the reverse. Employees were empowered to engage and work directly with customers, a condition that did not always exist under the old way of doing business. This change assisted the company in developing an open and welcoming environment in which there was freedom of movement with no unreasonable constraints. It also enabled customers and employees to nurture a close working relationship and to advance the image of Arbitron as being a progressive, customer-focused organization.

Consistent with the new management culture, teams were formed whereby employees could play a greater role in determinations that affected them and their relationship with the organization. The company consolidated and relocated their physical facilities during this time. These freshly renovated buildings were yet another powerful symbol that this was a dramatically new business, positioned for success. On arrival at the new buildings, a life safety and security team was formed. The charter of the team, which included a contract security officer supervisor, was to develop safety and security programs tailored to the new location. A decision was made that all previous policies and procedures were subject to review and challenge by the new employee team. Many of the original team members were invited to participate because they were "negative stakeholders," critical of past practice. Early meetings were described as being difficult and somewhat raucous and unfocused; although the rules had changed, some of the players had not.

Development of the overall guiding principle of people first, work in progress second, asset protection third was an essential ingredient to gaining team momentum. This easy-to-understand guiding principle became the standard against which all team proposals and outcomes were measured.

Strong leadership principles were successful in convincing most of the negative stakeholders that their participation and contributions would make a difference. However, the team was not to be used strictly as a forum to vent anger, debate opinions, or change history. Membership was a personal opportunity to help develop appropriate life safety and security programs consistent with the new culture. It was necessary that the team start thinking about the possibilities for improving all of the security programs, believing that their contributions made a difference, and learning that empowerment implies roving leadership and individual accountability.

The team leader recognized the importance of an early victory to solidify the team. This was accomplished with redesign of the company identification badge. Although this seemed like a small accomplishment, it was an employee-designed badge to be worn by all workers, customers, and visitors. The new badge reflected the professional image of the company. The feeling of achievement was evident within the team. It realized it could make a difference. If they could do this, what else might they accomplish? This pivotal first victory gave the team credibility and a sense of real value.

As Aribtron's life safety and security team matured, it took on progressively difficult issues. Agenda items were brought to the team by the leader, others were proposed by team members. Security post orders were reviewed and enhanced through team input. Members toured local companies that had installed state-of-the-art access-control equipment to learn of possible applications at Arbitron. Landscaping improvements to improve visibility of parking areas were undertaken, and security officer schedules and duty rotation were reviewed. Over time, an open-door policy was adopted by the team, and all employees were invited and encouraged to attend any regular meeting to present a specific concern or to make a suggestion.

A large portion of the responsibilities of the team concerns outsourcing of security services. The team carefully defines the scope of work to be undertaken, decides which organizations are solicited to tender a proposal, screens offers using a weighted criterion matrix, and conducts interviews that lead to final selection of a contractor. The intent of following such a logical process is to ensure that the supplier selected adds value to the highest degree possible and is embraced by the organization as a result of the team endorsement.

Although the charter of the team is very broad, some boundary conditions prohibit use of a team process. Examples include conducting investigations, exceeding budget constraints, reviewing personnel records, dealing with sexual harassment complaints, and other activities that require human resources or legal disciplines.

With the use of teamwork in its life safety and security programs, Arbitron enabled its employees to participate in decision making regarding asset protection. In addition to facilitating outsourcing initiatives, the life safety and security team enabled the organization to be more proactive in the design and execution of security programs and engage the entire workforce in the effort.

ADDING MEMBERS TO THE TEAM

As the team's work progresses, it may be necessary to add members who have special knowledge and skills. For example, an electronics engineer can provide advice regarding use of technological alternatives to security officer personnel. An information systems engineer might assist in determining which systems would be most adaptable to computerization or automation and help design them. It is important that a high degree of intellectual diversity be maintained within the team so that all alternatives are considered and the team members are continually encouraged to present new ideas. Selection of team members should depend not on who's available but on who is best qualified for the job.

As with any important task, the security project team may segment the assignment into sections that follow a logical sequence of proceedings. Each section also may be phased and specific goals and milestones established for the purpose of maintaining momentum and allowing changes at early stages. Each phase is addressed as an independent issue measurable against its objectives.

Security planning traditionally has been based on a predictable course of action that includes a security survey, system design, procurement, installation, and testing. These logical steps have worked well for decades in organizations interested in preventing security problems and analyzing the status of their security programs. In this process, emphasis is placed on an early evaluation of the existing status of the security program that may form a baseline against which proposed changes can be measured. In the work of the security project team, identification of problems and planning strategies become the initial concerns. An elaborate security survey is used as a supplementary device to assist in problem identification and planning for problem solving.

PROBLEM SOLVING

The first step is identification of a problem, which is usually qualitative in nature. The word *problem* is defined as a question proposed for solution or consideration. A company may not realize that a problem exists until something goes wrong or someone brings the problem to the attention of management. In many cases, the problem frequently is substantive and fortified with evidence. The problem also may be subjective. Although it may not be immediately substantiated with empirical evidence, it might constitute an area of concern that warrants further investigation and provides valuable results. The security project team is not constrained in the type of problems they approach, although a gradual step-by-step strategy is recommended. It would be more fruitful to resolve one puzzle at a time to fit the team's vision rather than to use the reverse course.

Determining underlying causes of a problem is an important consideration. If the root causes of problems are not fully addressed and definitively eliminated, the problems continue to exist beneath the surface and eventually reemerge regardless of the countermeasures used to mitigate them. It is necessary to differentiate that which appears to be a problem from actual symptoms of a problem. A symptom is described as an observable condition caused by a problem. For example, it may appear that there are not enough security officer personnel to perform required security patrols. An analysis reveals that the officers have non–security-related duties that consume their time. In this case, the inadequate number of security officers is the symptom and their assignment to duties unrelated to their main purpose is the problem. In many cases, examination of a symptom defines an obvious solution to a problem.

Problem identification is aided by a comprehensive security survey, which is used to identify the status of an existing program, locate and describe vulnerabilities, and define obstacles to an efficiently safe operation. In addition to helping identify problems, it contains solutions the team may consider. The value of a security survey is discussed in greater detail in Chapter 3.

Companies with no structured security unit but that envision a need for one because of operational or environmental changes that may pose concerns to the organization may use a team approach to aid in design of an organization that satisfies their concerns. However, absence of empirical information and a general lack of knowledge regarding security resources and how they might be deployed as an integrated system may place the team at a temporary disadvantage. These issues often can be resolved by engaging a professional independent security consultant to serve as an external advisor to the team and help guide them to successful achievement of their objectives.

The strategies to be used by the security project team to achieve their goals necessarily consider the unique philosophies and concerns of the company because they provide a sense of focus and guidance. Although these considerations are important, it also is important that the team not be constrained by them and be kept free from any bureaucratic restraints that impair the ability of the team to develop new approaches.

The team members also should not immediately consider financial issues as the main driving factor in their work. The main thrust of their efforts is to produce a long-range vision of the nature of security organization deemed ideal for the company. Of equal importance is determination that security functions can be outsourced and the manner in which quality can be achieved with the use of third-party contractors. If the cost of security becomes an issue in the team's initial pursuits, it is natural that it can become a negative influence that would diminish motivation and quickly defeat the creative purposes for which the team is assembled. The expense of implementing the final security program is an issue to be resolved as the latter phases of the overall security plan unfold. Expense does not have to be addressed by the security design team in the conceptual stages.

Several important considerations should provide positive direction for the security design team. Their objectives always should be consistent with their security vision. The vision is harmonious with the overall mission of the company and supports the strategic plans of the company to maintain its marketability now and in the future. Although the team might have the freedom to explore new ideas and different approaches, it is essential that it maintain clear and sharply defined attention to the full spectrum of adverse conditions that might reasonably be expected to threaten the assets of their company and to consider the various alternatives that might be used to safeguard those assets.

SUMMARY

The beneficial results of performance-oriented teams have been recognized throughout the industrial world for hundreds of years. This is because teams can surpass individuals as the primary performance unit within an organization. Although individual performance and accountability are values instilled in most people at early ages and have been credited for the development of the United States, they are not qualities antithetical to teamwork. A real team uses the individual skills, differences, and concerns of each team member to achieve collective strength and make a distinctive contribution. Teams represent one of the best ways to support the broad-based changes necessary for high performance within the organization. Executives who believe that characteristics such as quality, innovation, and cost effectiveness build continuing competitive advantage support the development of team performance.

The security design team can become an important influence in an organization because of its comprehensive involvement in most areas of the enterprise. The team's activities cut through interdepartmental networks and provide management with cost-effective and efficient methods of implementing its protective plans and visions. The team's work also serves as a tool to ensure an effective security operation that serves the demands of each operating unit.

The Top Ten Reasons to Outsource are included in this chapter. These are a guide to any team considering which internal functions or processes may be transferred to third-party experts and when to transfer them. They also may be used as general principles against which decisions about outsourcing may be tested.

3

Looking Inward

When a security project team undertakes the objective of determining which, if any, of the company security functions can be outsourced. It is necessary to have a comprehensive understanding of the company. Among its considerations, the team must know the company's purpose for existence, how it functions, its corporate culture, its strategic objectives, and why its assets require protection and by what means. To achieve this objective, the team analyzes the interactions between the security organization and other departments. This includes examination of the beneficial contributions, and any adversarial effects, of existing security systems, procedures, and programs on the functional relationships and interdependencies between other elements of the company. These insights provide information that gives value to the knowledge needed by the security project team to fulfill their objectives.

IDENTIFYING SECURITY REQUIREMENTS

While engaged in this internal assessment of security needs, the team should retain a mental recollection of the Ten Top Reasons to Outsource (see Chapter 2). This enables them to question each process and assists them in making a determination whether a process meets the criteria recommended for outsourcing. The team should bear in mind that perfect or absolute security is an unreachable state. Nothing is ever so well protected that it cannot be stolen, damaged, destroyed, or otherwise compromised by a dedicated foe or a natural catastrophe. Because the monetary and staffing costs of security constrain management efforts to achieve maximum protection for the entire business, the most logical path to follow is to determine the specific criticality and vulnerability of each area and allocate available resources and countermeasures accordingly. Special protection is provided for the most critical and vulnerable areas, whereas other areas of less importance and susceptibility may be given a lower level of attention appropriate to their value. This objective requires a distinct comprehension of the entire spectrum of threats the security program is designed to control and an understanding of the distinction between the terms *criticality* and *vulnerability*.

A *critical* area is one in which partial or complete loss of one or more components has an immediate and serious effect on the ability of the company to conduct business for an extended duration. Loss can be incurred through people problems, such as theft, sabotage, riots, fraud, and countless similar events, or through nonpeople problems, such as fire, floods, hurricanes, earthquakes, and other natural disasters.

There are various interpretations of the term *vulnerability* as applied to security management theories. For the purposes of this book, a more simplistic and traditional interpretation is offered. *Vulnerability* is the degree of susceptibility to which an organization may be exposed when hazards and threats are present that can cause loss, damage, or harm or otherwise adversely influence the operation of the concerned organization.

Security threats are acts or conditions, human or natural, that can result in personal injury or loss of life; damage, loss, or destruction of property; or disruption of the activities of the business. Severity of a threat depends on a number of variables, such as the type of business, the sensitivity of products or processes, physical layout and construction, geographic location, social, political and environmental influences, protective measures in effect, and similar features.

Before the security project team can envision an effective security program, it must determine the possibilities of the various types of interference that influence the capabilities of the organization from any and all sources. Unless these risks are clearly defined and understood, it is premature to identify areas of a security program that might be considered for outsourcing.

THE SECURITY SURVEY

The traditional security survey is the most effective tool for assisting the security project team in looking inward and determining the current state of security within the company. This is a formal and comprehensive on-site assessment of all aspects of the protective programs at the company and an evaluation of vulnerability and criticality factors and real or perceived threats and hazards that may effect it. A complete survey is similar to a systems analysis in that it entails explicit, in-depth review of each facet of the company's security processes and resources to determine the existing level of security integrity and to identify any deficiencies or excesses.

The security survey also helps define the level of protection needed to safeguard things that need protection and make judicious recommendations to improve overall security to a practical degree consistent with the requirements of the organization.

The quality of the results of a security survey is a matter of paramount value to the security design team. The team's entire mission depends on the information provided in the survey because it forms the foundation for the ultimate success of future efforts. The security survey is used to identify problems that may not have been previously defined and give alternative points of view and recommendations the security design team may consider to solve the problems in a cost-effective manner. Within these recommendations, the survey report provides information that assists the security project team in determining and selecting elements of the security program that might best be outsourced to contractors or retained as a proprietary service.

A comprehensive security survey is used as an aid to self-examination; analysis should not be limited to certain areas or concerns within the organization. When the scope of a survey is narrowed within the facility being studied, the team is denied essential information that relates to the dynamic interactions between all departments and other integrated processes appropriate to the objectives and goals of the organization and unquestionably to those of the security project team.

Regardless of size or structure, identifiable events within any business have some relation to one another and to the security programs of the company. A security survey might be nonproductive if its scope does not encompass the organization. For example, a limited survey can result in a positive action that provides adequate security for the department included in the survey but a negative reaction in a department not included in the study. This outcome might necessitate revision of routines and cause serious interruption of what may have previously been a smooth operation. The security design team must have sufficient information about all operations to ensure that any contemplated changes in the security organization mesh with or improve the overall security of the total organization.

It is virtually impossible to list the disciplines, subjects, and topics a comprehensive security survey should include. These are dictated by the size, structure, mission, and complexity of each organization. Within many firms, some of the chief factors to consider are the following:

1. Location, natural geography, and environment
2. Type of industry
3. General mission and objectives
4. Social and political influences
5. General business climate
6. Critical products, services, and locations
7. Management organization and strategic plans
8. Size and configuration of physical layout
9. Physical security resources and controls
10. Administrative security procedures, policies, and processes
11. Security management structure and organization
12. Emergency disaster and recovery plans
13. Internal functions and organizational interactions
14. Security awareness and attitudes

15. Applicability of legislative standards and regulations, including fire and safety
16. Effects and influence of bargaining units
17. Records reviews
18. Insurance, indemnity, and legal considerations
19. Customer expectations
20. Relation between management and employee expectations

These topics are not intended to be all inclusive. They are identified only as being representational of subjects to receive attention during the self-examination of an organization undergoing change. In addition to assisting the security project team in forming a master plan and determining whether and to what extent security services might be outsourced, other valuable benefits can be derived from use of the security survey approach, for example:

- It helps develop measures with which the team's goals can be evaluated
- It aids in development of security systems that mesh with the background of the firm for which the systems are designed
- It serves as a tool to enhance the competence of the security design team and assist management in its planning processes

The results of the survey are documented in a formal report that describes the deficiencies and excesses found and provides recommendations for improving the vulnerabilities uncovered. By studying the report of the security survey, the team develops a closer understanding of their own company and places the company in perspective with its environment. The report might explain why the company does some things in a certain way. For example, if the company has consistently avoided use of electronic access-control devices, the team should be warned that any change may be opposed, because the employees are used to long-standing procedures and have become comfortable with them. There always are people who do not like changing to a new system or who feel changing does not serve a worthwhile purpose. This may cause the team to encounter passive resistance in the future, especially during implementation of a new security system, unless they are cautious to approach the problem in such a way that the purpose of any change can be understood and made acceptable to those affected by it. If the team does not understand the background of the firm, it cannot relate day-to-day problems to the overall task, and efforts to effect change and achieve successful conclusions are impeded.

The information contained in the survey report aids the team in choosing the problems that are most relevant to their purpose and that deserve the highest priority. By establishing a logical sequence of strategic priorities concerning the problems identified, the team provides itself with a road map that points to where it is moving in the future.

THE TEAM'S REPORT

It is advisable that the team document the problems identified in a short report of their own that sets the stage for oral or written presentations to be communicated to management for judgment on the problem definition. Each written report may vary in subject matter, but it should generally include the following:

1. An introduction to the problem, including subject, scope, and definition
2. The criticality and vulnerability of the area being addressed
3. The problem and underlying causes
4. Relations between problems and their effects on other areas
5. Proposed solutions and recommendations
6. Economic factors, cost estimates, and benefits
7. The rationale and logic applicable to the recommendations, particularly if a recommendation is being made to outsource a function
8. A time table for implementation

These reports are the medium through which the security team communicates to management what it deems the problem to be, what it has found the causes to be, and what it has to offer in the way of solutions and recommendations.

WHO CONDUCTS THE SURVEY?

Performing a security survey is a time-consuming process in which the entire security environment of the organization is examined during normal working times, night-time hours, and other periods when the company may not be operational. In addition to the normal security-related skills needed to conduct a survey, it is necessary that the individuals involved in the survey have extensive knowledge of security standards and criteria, fire and safety codes, labor relations, statutory and regulatory standards, contractual agreements, legal implications, and similar types of laws and standards. Although the security project team may have some or all of these qualifications available to them, it is inadvisable that it undertake a security survey of its own facility. The team members are not expected to have the time necessary to complete a comprehensive survey or the complete objectivity and technical expertise to accomplish this task.

The security project team has several options at its disposal to perform a survey. It may be naturally disposed to select an in-house security manager if one is available for cost-savings considerations. Or the team may outsource the project to a third-party contractor. Although an in-house manager may possess all the desired skills and be a professional security practitioner, this manager's vested interest in the organization creates a potential conflict of interest. Although an in-house security manager would be invaluable as a source of historical information and other forms of assistance and support, it would be unfair to the company and the security manager to assign him or her to such a project. A more desirable alternative is to outsource the task to an independent professional security consultant, as discussed in Chapter 11.

The ability to look inward and determine what has been done in the past and relate those issues to the actions that must be taken to accommodate the present and to prepare for the future is a task that cannot be undertaken lightly. It must not be a superficial task but one in which much emphasis is placed on a comprehensive analysis of the entire organization to ensure that the strategic resources are protected.

The overall benefit of a security survey to the security project team is presentation of a broad picture of the existing security posture. Armed with this valuable information, the team is better equipped to proceed in its investigation of the security programs and posture of the company as they affect whether it is appropriate to outsource security functions or retain them within the organization. There is a commonly held theory that from the time of conception, everything has a natural tendency to evolve downward to its lowest level unless it is continually supported and upheld. It is imperative that the person responsible for managing the security program constantly test and examine all facets of the program to ensure that all systems are functioning as intended and that it maintains pace with operational changes of the organization.

The function of the security project design team does not end at this point. In a position with perspective, the team may begin to concentrate on the path forward. As it proceeds, the team should continually remind itself of the Top Ten Reasons to Outsource, because these reasons are part of the objectives.

SUMMARY

This chapter discusses some of the methods a project security team might use to obtain information regarding the existing security posture of the organization and assess future security requirements. It also addresses use of a comprehensive security survey to assist in reaching that determination. The survey includes an overall evaluation of the security program, describes how it operates, defines its processes, and identifies its relationships with internal and external customers. These are all important elements of information. Equally important is that the survey aids the team in visualizing the role of the security organization and its contributions and connections to the core competencies of the organization. Such information is vital to the team as it pursues the issue of whether outsourcing some or all security functions is in the best interests of the organization.

4

Looking Outward

Having used a security survey and its own efforts to acquire the information necessary to gain perspective on its organization's security operations, the security project team proceeds further in determining whether to outsource any or all of the security functions beneficial to the interests of the company. This chapter discusses several issues in the security project team's examination of the core competencies of the company and the influence on outsourcing of security services. It also poses questions the security project team eventually has to answer in making decisions regarding outsourcing.

EXAMINING CORE COMPETENCIES

The core competencies of the company and the various influences that affect decisions must be examined. Questions such as the following must be asked:

- Will outsourcing the security organization enhance the company's ability to concentrate more fully on productivity, quality, and profit making and improve its ability to excel over competitors and become a leader in its field?
- Is there evidence that a third-party contractor can provide security services equal to or better than those provided by the internal security organization?
- Can a security contractor contribute to the core competencies of the company substantial intellectual, technological, or other advanced resources and services or otherwise improve marketability?
- Are there liabilities or similar exposures inherent in the maintenance of an internal security organization that can be eliminated or mitigated by transferring or sharing them with an external security service provider?
- Are there functions now performed by the security organization that can be performed effectively by other internal departments?
- If it is determined that it is essential to the core competencies of the company and should not be outsourced, can the security organization perform additional responsibilities now being performed by other departments? For example, a company has a security staff charged with the responsibility of

conducting security inspections. It may also have a separate safety staff that performs safety inspections and perhaps a third unit that undertakes internal audits. Can these functions be combined within one smaller group and be performed with equal or better results at less cost?

These questions coincide with some of the Top Ten Reasons to Outsource, which ultimately drive the actions of the security project team.

REVERSE OUTSOURCING

While studying whether it is appropriate to outsource security services, the security project team might also consider whether internal security services have capabilities that might be outsourced to others. In examining the core competencies of the company, the team might spend time brainstorming whether the security organization might supplement or become more closely integrated with those competencies by outsourcing its services to other companies. If it is determined that an internal security organization does provide positive and needed support to the goals and objectives of the company, the security project team may question whether the internal security organization has specialized resources or expertise the company might market to other organizations. A few examples include security consultations and audits, security awareness indoctrinations, security officer training, security systems integration assistance, and other services depending on the scope of skills or resources of the company's security staff. If the team considers this an initiative to pursue, it can plant the seed for developing a new company culture, or at least expanding the current one.

For the purposes of this discussion, let us assume that the security project team chooses to take this initiative several steps farther. By virtue of an analysis of the internal security organization provided by the security survey, they now should have a grasp of the various processes performed by the security organization and its capabilities and competence. The analysis also might provide information that suggests the organization can have marketable capabilities. The team is faced with additional questions. Among them are the following:

- What differentiates the company's security organization from others, and what resources do they have that might not be available in other enterprises?
- Are these services of such a nature that they are not likely to exist in other companies?
- Are these services of such a nature that they would be needed by other companies?
- Can the potential market by readily identified? What is it, where is it, and how can it best be reached?
- What is the local, regional, and national competition in providing these services, and can that competition be overcome?

- Would substantial capital or operational expenditures be required to market these services?
- Would the provision of these services reduce the operational costs of the internal security function or make it self-sustaining?
- Would management support such an endeavor?
- What other external and internal support would this effort require, such as marketing, advertising, accounting, and legal?
- Can any supportable projection be formed regarding the level of profit such an effort would bring to the company?
- Would provision of these services to external companies improve the organization's ability to enter new markets or establish relationships that would bring new business opportunities to the company?

Many of these questions can be answered with market and feasibility studies the team examines and weighs carefully before any recommendation to implement the plan can be put before management. The team also has to use a great deal of imagination and creative thinking in considering whether this initiative is an option for the company. Although it is good to concentrate on established core competencies of an organization, these are not always so well cast in stone that they cannot be changed or refocused with creative thinking on the part of the team.

OUTSOURCING TRENDS

A question being asked is how far the trend toward outsourcing will continue as an alternative to employment of internal security support services. Studies by the Outsourcing Institute predicted that outsourcing grew by 35% during 1996 and 1997. Of course, these figures included all nature of services being contracted to third parties. Although not specifically differentiated, it is assumed that security services were included in that prediction. However, in *Security Management: Business Strategies for Success,* Dennis Dalton gives us more specific data when he states that U.S. Department of Labor estimates indicate that almost 60% of companies that use security services rely heavily on contract providers.

The aforementioned indicators reflect a growing trend among companies of all sizes to peel away everything but the core. They also show that many companies are finding that outsourcing can be a successful endeavor; otherwise the numbers would be declining or at least leveling off instead of continuing to increase. Although many notable successes are associated with outsourcing, some companies have transferred various tasks to outside contractors and found the results to be far less than anticipated in terms of both cost and productivity. They have returned to the use of in-house staffs. Others have had mixed results but continue to cling to outsourced services because of lower costs. Still others claim great success with contract service providers. It is difficult to discern definitively the predominant reasons for such a wide divergence of experiences within these companies, which represent a broad spectrum of businesses, including Fortune 500 corporations and small companies. The causes can be as endless as the number of varied services being contracted. The effect depends heavily on the culture, mission, and management expectations of the user organization. Every company has its own peculiarities and requirements that differentiate it from the rest. A strategy that is vastly successful in one organization may be less so in others.

The trend to outsource all types of services is increasing. This gives rise to the assumption that it may be the answer to cutting costs and redefining the manner in which many companies do business in the future. When outsourcing action is taken on the basis of information gathered in comprehensive studies of services and processes to be contracted to third parties, there is a greater chance that it will succeed. Conversely, when a company engages in outsourcing merely because it works for another company and makes that decision without any objective study or knowledge, the results may be less than expected.

STAYING IN OR GOING OUT

There are many good reasons for a company to choose to retain an internal service, even one not part of the core competencies of the business. For example, a defense contractor that produces volumes of classified material in accordance with contractual requirements may wish to retain its own printing and publication department in which the employees possess the government personnel security clearances required to have access to such material. In many areas, it may be difficult to locate a third-party resource with the capability of protecting classified material or with cleared personnel to whom this material may be disclosed. In this event, it might be imprudent to attempt to outsource this function.

There are also many good reasons why a company may choose to retain internal services, because it is deemed to work best for them. However, services being performed that are not entirely consistent with the core competencies of an organization may not be the panacea many managers and executives perceive them to be. The security project team must focus carefully on security requirements relevant to the organization and supportable with research findings. For example, at some point within its deliberations, the security project team may focus attention on whether a security officer service should become a part of the company security program. If the team decides this is a viable pursuit, the two main options are employing a proprietary security officer force or employing a force provided by a contractor, because these are the sources most frequently used. It might be appropriate to discuss some of the perceived differences between two alternatives. For this discussion, the terms *security officer force* and *protective force* should be considered synonymous.

The traditional advantages of an in-house security officer force most often stated are: (1) there is an expectation of permanency, stability, quality, and loyalty; (2) training can be held to uniform standards consistent with organizational requirements; and (3) individual performance and evaluation in accordance with prescribed policies and discipline can be controlled and administered by company management. Personnel selection traditionally was an unshared prerogative, and the security officer force became an interactive part of the entire security organization. Another proposed benefit of an in-house security officer force was that in many states an industrial protective force could be commissioned with special police authority that gave them the power to detain and arrest persons engaged in criminal activity on company property. In some places, the numbers of industrial police working at business facilities outweighed those of the municipal police.

Whereas proponents of proprietary security officer forces may agree that the cost of a contract service is less than that of an in-house force, the question of performance and productivity remains as concerns because of old perceptions of the contract security industry, that is a "rent-a-cop" or "we versus them" mentality. As outsourcing became prevalent, many companies such as General Electric, Allied Signal, and other smaller organizations (many of them using the team approach) started to examine methods by which they might reduce security costs. As a result, they began divesting themselves of the proprietary guard forces that existed within enterprises and replaced them with contractor-provided security officers. The main purpose was to reduce operating costs, make capital funds available for other purposes, and provide a greater focus on core competencies.

BEING ON THE SAME TRAIN

Although chief executive officers are constantly seeking ways to reduce cost, they are rarely willing to sacrifice protection of assets or have the security integrity of the organization diminished unreasonably. Consequently, security contractors are in a position in which they have to ensure that high-quality services are provided that equal or exceed those of the services they replace. They must also be agreeable to adjusting to the culture of the client's organization and to taking all measures necessary to ensure a high level of customer satisfaction.

Security contractors must provide services that enhance the corporate image and contribute to the objectives of the client. They are challenged to increase their level of professionalism through continuous improvement, quality service, management, and performance. In other words, to be successful, they have to be on the same train as the client!

The security project team is faced with many thought-provoking issues when deciding which type of service is most beneficial to the organization. In making this decision, the team is encouraged to weigh the requirements of its organization against the alternatives. The team should ask, Is there a compelling and exceptional reason why a proprietary security officer force can provide benefits and advantages a contract service cannot, if the special requirements were specifically defined in a statement of work for the contractor? To this extent, the statement of work becomes a very important tool with which the security project team works.

SUMMARY

This chapter provides information and concepts that take the project security team closer to the point at which it begins to engage itself with the actual tactics of outsourcing. It discusses trends of outsourcing and its importance in the future well-being of organizations and questions whether that concept is a cure-all for the challenge of businesses to remain competitive. The chapter also brings the team to the point at which it considers the tasks a contractor is expected to perform and the manner in which quality is to be assured.

5

Statement of Work

This chapter outlines suggestions for development of a statement of work for outsourcing security services. The example is for a security officer force, but the standards identified apply to other types of services required to protect the assets of an organization. More specific services are discussed in later chapters, but the basic considerations are similar to those identified here.

LAYING THE FOUNDATION

It is prudent to examine a few of the reasons why some companies are successful in their efforts to outsource security functions and obtain quality services and why others are less fortunate. Some of the fundamental causes that lead to a more successful relationship between the user organization and the contractor are as follows:

1. *Planning.* The user firm has developed a comprehensive plan based on a full analysis of its security requirements and has determined it is more appropriate to outsource certain well-defined security functions.
2. *Resources.* A study has been made of the resources in the immediate area, and there are contractors available with capability to provide the required services in sufficient numbers to be competitive.
3. *Requirements.* The user has carefully prepared a comprehensive request for proposal accompanied by a specific statement of work and submitted these to a minimum of five potential bidders. The statement of work designates a contract monitor, usually the firm's security manager or a designee.
4. *Evaluation.* All proposals are evaluated with regard to understanding of the statement of work, technical qualifications, managerial capabilities, and cost considerations. Contractors who clearly fail to pass through any of these gates should be eliminated from further consideration.
5. *Negotiation.* Negotiations begin and questions regarding each proposal are prepared, preferably by the security design team. They are returned

to the bidder for clarification in a best and final bid or are asked of the bidder in the event of an oral presentation. No question or concern should be left unresolved.

6. *Credibility.* An investigation of the finalists' financial status, performance history, litigation involvement, professional standing, management background, and other facets of the business should be conducted and references carefully evaluated.

7. *Selection.* A successful bidder is chosen on the basis of a careful evaluation of the level of cost compared with the perceived abilities of the contractor to fulfill the contractual obligation to deliver the quality of service that meets the expectations of the user.

8. *Award.* The successful bidder is awarded the contract, and the service begins.

9. *Postaward monitoring.* A contract monitor continues to evaluate the service, immediately resolve problems, and act as the user organization's liaison between the company and the contractor's management to ensure compliance with all contractual stipulations and specifications.

These nine points are discussed in detail later. They are stated at this point to exemplify the basic principles that may be applied to establishing the foundation on which a harmonious relationship with a contractor may be created regardless of the form or strategies on which the relationship is based. These considerations are the minimum elements for a successful client-contractor relationship. Other actions can be included according to the business structure of the user.

CREATIVE RELATIONSHIPS WITH VENDORS

In *Security Management: Business Strategies for Success,* Dennis Dalton describes four different methods of outsourcing, as follows:

- The traditional vendor relationship
- The preferred vendor relationship
- The strategic partner relationship
- The strategic alliance relationship

Each of these strategies involves progressive levels of relationships that might exist between the client and the contractor. The continuum begins with the *traditional buyer-seller* arrangement, in which the contractor performs only the usual routine tasks at the lowest cost. The *preferred vendor* relationship is one in which the vendor is perceived to offer value-added services and capabilities under a quality-driven program, and the client is willing to use these services on a multiyear contract basis. In a *strategic partner* relationship, both parties agree to enter into a long-term arrangement that provides shared benefits to each party in terms of business growth, continual improvement, problem resolution and communication. The highest form of a contractor-client relationship is the new concept of a *strategic alliance* relationship in which both parties seek a cooperative and harmonious arrangement in which they agree to integrate the commercial and technical aspects of their businesses for mutual benefit. Regardless of the level of relationship sought between user and contractor, the same nine basic elements for a successful association remain substantially the same.

IDENTIFYING REQUIREMENTS

After thorough study and assessment of its internal structure and after careful consideration, a company determines that it is more practical and cost effective to outsource a security officer service rather than to employ an in-house force. The study also has disclosed the number of posts to be staffed, and a schedule of work hours has been formulated. The duties security officers are expected to perform have been carefully defined, as have insurance requirements, training certifications, personnel qualifications, supervisory structure, procedures, anticipated costs, and other matters relevant to implementation of the security officer force and its performance. Defense contractors performing on classified contracts may have the added concern of personnel security clearances, which must be provided by the vendor if the client requires them. The study also identifies any other security services the organization wants the contractor to perform, such as executive protection, investigations, courier duties, monitoring international travel information, or other functions the client cannot perform easily and inexpensively for itself.

SEARCHING FOR VENDORS

The user firm prepares an exacting statement of work and request for proposal to be submitted to potential bidders. Depending on the numbers of contractors available to the company, the firm is advised to select no less than five vendors to maintain an appropriate level of competition. It is unwise to submit requests for proposal to more than ten vendors, because evaluation of these extra proposals is time consuming and counterproductive. The user firm conducts a search for potential contractors within the area in which the company is located. Care should be taken to ensure that the management offices of the contractor are situated within a radius of no more than one hour's driving time of the client's facility. This is to ensure that contractor management liaison, supervision, and support can be provided in a timely manner.

DEFINING REQUIREMENTS TO VENDORS

The written statement of work defines in detail the requirements and specifications of the work to be performed by the selected vendor. This documentation is the basis for all activity related to the bidding process and allows the user firm intelligent selection of a successful bidder. At minimum, the statement of work should include the following:

1. Specific service requirements
2. Staffing and equipment requirements
3. Training requirements
4. Performance standards
5. Wages and benefits to be paid
6. Administrative procedures
7. Insurance, licensing, indemnification
8. Default penalties
9. Termination clause
10. Description and floor plans of the facility to be protected

SPECIFIC REQUIREMENTS

The specific service requirements section of the statement of work is the blueprint for the security services being provided. It defines all details of the tasks to be performed and allows bidders to determine their requirements and qualifications to respond to the request for proposal. Absence of this valuable information places bidders at a disadvantage to the extent that they do not fully understand what resources they must possess and what tasks they are expected to perform. They consequently are caused to make their own perceptions regarding things the customer is requesting and draw erroneous conclusions that may result in a flawed proposal.

All security-related operational duties should be clearly outlined in the specific service requirements section of the statement of work. For example, the outline includes a list of instructions relative to each post and defines the nature of the duties and activities to be performed on each shift at that particular assignment. If the security officer personnel are expected to enforce company work policies, labor rules, or other policies and procedures applicable to company employees, these rules should be included. The bidders should have as much information as is necessary for them to recognize and understand the requirements of a client so that they can provide a comprehensive response to the request for proposal.

STAFFING

The statement of work includes staffing requirements and defines the specific hours of coverage by posts and shifts. For example,

Post No.	Description	Shift	Hours per week
1	Main duty desk	24 hours 7 days	168.0
2	Alarm and closed-circuit TV console	24 hours 7 days	168.0
3	Employee entrance	24 hours 7 days	168.0
4	Restricted area entrance	24 hours 7 days	168.0
5	Internal foot patrol	24 hours 7 days	168.0
6	Exterior mobile patrol	24 hours 7 days	168.0
7	Photo ID center	0800+1600 M+F	40.0
8	Main receptionist	0800+1600 M+F	40.0

Total weekly staffing requirement is 1,088 hours.

Many security service providers adhere to the use of military ranks and titles for their employees. For the purposes of a statement of work, the user firm may wish to use this method to identify the levels of personnel to be assigned to each post and shift. This aids bidders in determining the costs of staffing for each post. An example is as follows:

Post No.	Shift	Staff Member
1	0800–1600	Security force captain
1	1600–2400	Shift lieutenant
1	2400–0800	Shift lieutenant
2	All	Console sergeant
3	All	Security officers
4	All	Security officers
5	All	Patrol officers
6	All	Patrol officers
7	0800–1600	Security officers
8	0800–1600	Receptionist

TRAINING

Training is a vital consideration in the preparation of a statement of work. The primary mission of security personnel is the protection of persons and the safeguarding of a company's other assets. The advanced security technology used within many industries increases the need that security officers responsible for monitoring or operating technical equipment, consoles, intrusion and fire detection systems, and similar systems be competent and qualified to fulfill the function effectively and knowledgeably. In addition to the need that the security officer have some computer literacy, it is essential that he or she have the ability to make intelligent decisions and take appropriate action when dealing with emergencies or other adverse conditions.

Certification Requirements

The statement of work being prepared by the client should include certification requirements for all security officers being assigned to the facility. These include the minimum following topics:

1. Basic fire-fighting techniques
2. Advanced first aid training
3. Cardiopulmonary resuscitation
4. Motor vehicle operator permit when required
5. Firearms qualifications and training when required

The contractor should be required to provide within a specified time period, usually not to exceed 30 days of the award of contract, certificates or other documentation of training from registered or otherwise approved training resources. All contractual training requirements should be satisfied in a timely manner and appropriate entries made in an individual's training records. Failure to comply with this requirement should compel the contractor to pay a default penalty.

Specialized Training

A client may have unique concerns, such as hazardous materials, pharmaceutical products, or classified information, that require special protection. This necessitates specialized training and familiarization on the part of security officers to safeguard the material. These concerns should be identified in detail within the training requirements section of the statement of work together with any regulatory requirements or standards that may apply and with which the security officers should be acquainted.

The statement of work should make reference to any company policies and procedures the security officers are expected to enforce. These are usually defined in an employee's handbook or other procedural documents to which the officers must have access on assignment. They should be designated required reading as a condition of assignment.

On-the-Job Training

Many large private security contractors have an in-house staff to provide basic security officer training to new employees and advanced training to managers. They provide fundamental instructions to the guards through a variety of media that give the guards the preliminary education to help them perform their duties. The number of hours of on-the-job training a trainee must receive can be specified in the statement of work. This may vary from 8 to 40 hours depending on the complexity of the assignment. This training acquaints security officers with conditions that will confront them on an assignment. Because the concerns of each client are vastly different, it is necessary for security officers to become almost instantly and intimately acquainted with all aspects of the facility to which they are assigned. This can be a herculean task for someone with the responsibilities of a security officer.

Security Procedures

The client can ameliorate some of the problems associated with on-the-job training by providing written instructions in the nature of post orders, which define specific duties according to posts and shifts. The client also should provide a manual of approved security procedures for security personnel to follow in discharging their duties and to give guidance to resolve questions and problems. Although it is not necessary to include a security manual with the statement of work and request for proposal, it is appropriate to discuss briefly the value of the manual. The security manual is a critical training aid to which security officers may refer while performing their assigned tasks. This manual should contain all rules, regulations, and expectations relating to security officers' performance and consolidate memorandums and directives that are relevant to the security officers' work.

A Security Manual for Security Officers

The following is a suggested format for a security officers' manual:

I.   General. The user makes a general statement regarding the purpose of the security officer force, its authority, and the objectives the security organization are expected to meet.

II.   Emergency telephone numbers and points of contact

III.   Organization
      A. Contract security organization
      B. Client organization

IV.   Security officer training
    A. Security manual (required reading)
    B. Preassignment training
    C. On-the-job or site-specific indoctrination
    D. Knowledge testing
    E. In-service training
    F. Specialized training

V.   Security officers' rules and regulations
    A. Appearance
    B. Rules of conduct
    C. Discipline

VI.   General duties
    General orders

VII.   Security equipment
    A. Weapons (when applicable)
    B. Protective equipment and proper use
    C. Two-way radio equipment and procedures
    D. Public address and emergency reporting systems and procedures
    E. Closed-circuit television and recorders
    F. Electronic security systems, alarms, remote control devices
    G. Surveillance and detection devices
    H. Vehicle care and use
    I. Other equipment as applicable

VIII.   Parking areas
    A. Violations
    B. Automobile accident investigation on company property
    C. Vehicle theft
    D. Traffic direction
    E. Assistance to disabled vehicles
    F. Actions during snow or other natural storms

IX.   Security plan compatibility
    A. Perimeter fence and gate control
    B. Outlying post inspection

X.   Personnel and vehicle control
    A. Personnel identification procedures
    B. Vehicle registration
    C. Visitor control

XI.   Report writing

XII.   Communication
    A. Radio
    B. Telephone

        C. Fax machine

XIII. Fire protection
        A. Training
        B. Drills
        C. Fire equipment location and use
        D. Communication

XIV. Medical support
        A. Emergency treatment
        B. Response
        C. On-site medical facility
        D. Medical transportation in company vehicle
        E. Obtaining emergency medical services
        F. Reporting

XV. Emergency control procedures
        A. Definition
        B. Classification of emergencies
        C. On-site organization
        D. Security and safety interface plan
        E. Natural disasters
        F. Bomb threats
        G. Civil or internal disorders
        H. Labor disputes and disturbances
        I. Evacuation plans and actions

XVI. Alarm and intrusion detection systems
      Actions to be taken by security personnel

XVII. Rules of conduct for client employees

XVIII. Authority and jurisdiction of security officer personnel (local and state laws apply)
        A. Arrest and apprehension
        B. Physical searches in relation to inspection of hand-carried property
        C. Law enforcement liaison
        D. Delivery of warrants or subpoenas for company personnel
        E. Vehicle searches

XIX. Post instructions

XX. Special instructions

XXI. Site fire and evacuation plans

XXII. Facility layout plan

XXIII. Other sections as necessary

Post Instructions

Post instructions are critical to security officer force operations. They constitute the specific directions for the security personnel to follow while performing duties on each post on each shift. Each instruction should deal with a single subject, which should allow for revision or cancellation of outdated orders or changes in requirements. Instructions should be as concise as possible. They are action documents describing how, when, and what the guard must do in each predictable instance. These instructions should be simply written in basic English on the lowest readability level possible. Because reading time is related to reading comprehension, the longer it takes to read an instruction the less likely it is to be accurately understood and remembered. Instructions should be indexed in detail to allow rapid location of relevant provisions. Only instructions relevant to each post should be maintained at the post. A master copy of all instructions is usually retained by supervisory personnel.

PERFORMANCE STANDARDS

Performance standards must be included in the statement of work. These specifications define the level of performance anticipated by the client and place a contractual obligation on the provider to supply quality services. The client should stipulate the prerogative to exclude from assignment any security officers who are deemed incompetent, negligent, insubordinate, or otherwise objectionable or unsuitable to perform services at the facility. A client should be advised that whenever a contractor employee is dismissed from a facility for cause, all company-issued property, such as keys, key cards, and identification cards, should be recovered and accounted for. The individual should be barred from returning to the facility for any reason except at the company's convenience. Client cannot compel a contractor to discharge an employee for any reason; they may only exclude an unacceptable individual from assignment to their facilities.

In the event a new security contractor is assuming a contract previously performed by another vendor, the client may, at its discretion, nominate certain incumbent guards who have demonstrated a high level of performance and whom the user wishes to retain. In most instances, the contractor is quite willing to hire these persons to satisfy the client and to maintain a core of facility-trained guards who are familiar with the client's premises, infrastructure, and operations. These persons are particularly useful if the client uses complex computerized security systems or performs other esoteric duties for which the guards must be trained. However, when incumbent security officers are to be employed by a successor contractor, they must meet the background requirements of the new employer. For example, the new contractor may have pre-employment drug testing whereas the former contractor may not.

Contractors should be required by the statement of work to perform comprehensive background investigations on each employee selected to work at a client's facility. The investigation should determine suitability and qualifications, a clean arrest record, an unremarkable driving record, an acceptable credit report, and other personal qualities and lifestyles that indicate integrity, reputability, dependability, and the capability to act decisively and responsibly and use tact during interactions with other people.

Physical standards should be established that ensure all selected guard personnel are able to cope with the mental and physical demands of the work to be performed. Security guards should be free from recurring illnesses, communicable diseases, physical defects, and hearing impairments. A guard's weight should not exceed 3.25 times his or her height in inches. Visual acuity should be correctable to a 20/20 standard. The physical and mental qualifications of a security guard are an important consideration for a client because they can make the difference between whether the company maintains a high level of reputation and operation or is jeopardized by a flawed personal action. It is important that the client realize the Americans with Disabilities Act has to be considered and that reasonable accommodation may be required by law.

To maintain a level of quality within a contract, the client may want to include a requirement for quality assurance in the statement of work. The contractor pledges to commit to a quality assurance program and outlines proposed actions to ensure measurable value-added service and continued improvement throughout the contract period. Including this stipulation in a statement of work provides the contractor with an excellent opportunity to identify its quality and productivity improvement initiatives and define how these visions may blend with those of the client or be consistent with them.

WAGES AND BENEFITS

Companies that desire a quality guard service should be prepared to pay the additional cost as opposed to those willing to accommodate a minimum-wage watch or lowest category of security officer. This added expense is an investment that adds value to the service and provides tangible returns from an asset-protection point of view. As a rule, all guard services draw from the same pool of available personnel; only the quality of the people within the pool is different. To ensure that the vendor supplies well-qualified employees, wage standards should be at least competitive with other quality firms. The client firm is advised to establish a standard of minimum wages to be paid to guard personnel and a schedule by which the wages might be increased over the term of the contract depending on level of performance. These standards should be included in the statement of work. An example follows:

Title	Start	90 Days	1 Year	2 Years
Guard captain	$11.50	$12.00	$13.00	$14.00
Lieutenant	$10.50	$11.00	$12.00	$13.00
Sergeant	$9.50	$10.00	$11.00	$12.00
Patrol officer	$9.00	$9.50	$10.50	$11.50
Receptionist	$9.00	$9.50	$10.00	$11.00
Security officer	$8.50	$9.00	$9.50	$10.00

Because wage standards vary according to geographic area, the user should conduct a wage survey of comparable organizations within the area to determine a wage level appropriate to the requirements.

Many companies still insist on procuring security contract services on the basis of lowest cost. They might be inclined to refrain from establishing an equitable wage rate in a statement of work. These firms depend entirely on the contractor to provide wage costs in the proposal. They then select a vendor based solely on lowest price, regardless of the qualifications of the personnel being provided or the level of management exercised over the contract by the vendor. In these cases, the security service supplier may provide less-qualified people at minimum wage with few if any benefits. This results in a high attrition rate within the security officer force. The rapid turnover of personnel causes deterioration of officers' knowledge and familiarity with the facility and any training standards initially anticipated by the client, because knowledgeable guards are constantly being replaced with those who are untrained.

Security officer supervision often is negligible, and management liaison between the client and contractor usually occurs only when problems emerge that are of such proportion to demand managerial intervention by the contractor. The downward evolution of the security program continues as knowledge and service decline until they reach their lowest point. The high risks assumed by both parties become a reality as asset-protection resources are jeopardized. This scenario is not unusual and is being perpetuated by organizations that do not consider the value the security organization provides to a company or lacks knowledge of the techniques that might be used to obtain quality security service at reasonable cost.

The statement of work should stipulate the manner in which holiday pay should be paid. In the private security industry, the following six traditional holidays are observed and paid as overtime:

New Years Day
Memorial Day
Independence Day
Labor Day
Thanksgiving Day
Christmas

If the client wants the contractor's on-site guards to observe the same holidays as the user organization, this should be included in the statement of work. Holiday wages should be charged to the client only as they occur.

Bidders should be advised that vacation pay should not be computed in their rate but should be charged only at the time the payment is made to the employee, for the following reasons:

1. Vacation pay is payable only to full-time employees, usually after 1 year of employment. If a guard terminates employment before the anniversary date, the vacation pay is not always given to the employee but is retained by the contractor as additional profit.
2. Some guard providers may suspend 1 day or more vacation time as a disciplinary measure if a guard commits an infraction. The accrual for any vacation denied the security officer is retained as extra profit.

Overtime charges should be billed when it is explicitly authorized and stated in writing by the user. For example, if the client is having a special function and wants a particular security officer who normally works a 40-hour week to perform a specific duty at the affair during which overtime is incurred, overtime in this case is acceptable. However, if a security officer is retained on a shift because normal relief is not immediately available, overtime charges for that officer should not be accepted. Overtime and holiday rates should be computed as a straight-time rate plus one-half wage with payroll tax.

If the client is willing to authorize medical, hospitalization, and life insurance benefits for security officer personnel in excess of that provided by the contractor, the type and scope of benefits should be stated and identified clearly in the statement of work. In some cases, a client may stipulate the dollar amount of benefits authorized, such as $1.50 per hour per individual authorized for benefits.

ADMINISTRATIVE ISSUES

The client should use the statement of work as a clear definition of all expectations of work performance and service. Included should be other topics such as identifying equipment, forms, communication devices, office space, and any other material to be provided by the client and what the contractor is expected to provide. Administrative issues must be addressed. These normally include legal matters, insurance requirements, indemnification, records and reports, and appointment of a company contract monitor to act as the primary point of contact between the client and the contractor. The monitor has full authority to monitor the contract operation, inspect billing records, make adjustments, issue change orders, authorize overtime, and resolve all contractual problems, including termination of the contract if conditions warrant such action.

A user may define the manner and format in which the proposal is to be presented. This normally includes a management portion, a technical section, and a cost proposal. Each portion of the proposal should be weighted in terms of importance to the evaluation of the proposal. A sample might be as follows:

Management section	30%
Technical section	20%
Cost proposal	50%

Bidders might be invited to submit an alternative plan for consideration. For example, a bidder who has an innovative plan regarding a certain requirement of the statement of work that might reduce cost or provide a better service to the client should have the opportunity to describe that idea to the client. This is an excellent opportunity for the contractor to be creative and provide value-added concepts to the company's security program.

The request for proposal specifies that a bidders' conference and site inspection are scheduled. All bidders who want to submit proposals are required to attend this conference and inspection. The client should exclude from bidding all contractors not in attendance. The conference includes an in-depth review of the statement of work, and any questions the attendees might have are answered. The site inspection consists of a thorough guided tour of the facility and grounds to acquaint the bidders with the physical security, technology, layout, and configuration of the organization. The bidders' conference is a valuable tool for users and for contractors. It enables all prospective bidders to hear the same things at the same time. They are provided with ample opportunity to ask questions and to be provided with answers that allow submission of intelligent proposals. The conference also eliminates the possibility of any excuses that a contractor was not aware of a particular requirement.

DEFAULT PENALTIES

Adjustment of compensation for failed work performance or noncompliance with the stipulation cited in the statement of work should be included as a part of the contract. Because the client has indicated an expectation of high-quality services, there should be an equitable adjustment of contract charges that fairly reflects reduced value of performance. The client may prepare a matrix to be included in the statement of work that defines acts that constitute a default of contractual obligations on the part of the contractor and stipulates a specific sum of money to be subtracted from payment for each default. When such deductions are to be made, the client should advise the contractor in writing of the intent to deduct payment and identify the specific cause for the penalty.

The following conditions are examples of circumstances of sufficient severity to warrant imposition of a financial penalty:

1. Failure to provide a security guard for a post or shift as specified in the statement of work
2. Failure to pay contractual wages and benefits
3. Failure to meet prescribed insurance requirements
4. Assignment of guards without prescribed training certifications, licenses, or permits required by the statement of work or local or state laws
5. Assignment of guards without personnel security clearances as required by the statement of work and federal regulation
6. Assignment of guards who possess a physical or mental impairment, addiction to or use of illegal substances, criminal conviction of a serious nature, or any other condition prohibited by the statement of work or otherwise reasonably deemed by the client to be inconsistent with the client's best interests and that should have been known or suspected by the contractor
7. Failure to maintain complete and accurate records of all hours worked by each security officer for which payment is computed on the basis of actual hours worked
8. Failure to provide a properly uniformed security guard
9. Failure to replace a particular security guard within 8 hours on verbal request of an authorized company representative, depending on work requirements
10. Failure to furnish prescribed equipment and material necessary for the performance of services prescribed in the statement of work
11. Failure to investigate any reported act of wrongdoing by guard personnel
12. Failure to respond or act on any written or oral complaint from an authorized company representative
13. Failure to verify legal immigration status of any non-U.S. citizen being assigned to the work site
14. Failure to comply with training requirements stipulated in the statement of work

TERMINATION CLAUSE

Each statement of work should contain a termination clause that defines the terms and conditions in which the contract may be terminated by either party before expiration of the term of contractual performance. This clause defines issues such as the following:

- Termination by client without cause
- Termination by default or material breech of contractual obligations by either party

- Termination for bankruptcy, receivership, insolvency, failure to maintain licenses or insurance, or similar actions on the part of the contractor
- Including written notices of intent to terminate and time limits for submitting such notices
- Compensation obligations as a result of contract cancellation

TRANSITION TEAMS

If a security guard contract has been awarded to a new vendor, the client may consider discouraging use of a transition team of new security officers, except in compelling circumstances in which the vendor may not have trained personnel available to assign to the contract. For the purposes of this discussion, the term *transition team* refers only to the individual security guards being assigned to post duties and should not be construed to include the contractor's management staff responsible for ensuring a smooth transition of the security operation.

A transition team is usually a group of guards who are young, well groomed, attractive, and attentive persons who appear to represent a high-quality service and are impressive to the new client. Over time, however, a degenerative metamorphosis occurs. The guards no longer seem quite as trim, attentive, or intelligent as they first appeared. Their sparkle and luster appears to fade, and they no longer have the enthusiastic bearing and appearance of before. The reason is simply because they are not the same people. The transition team has been gradually withdrawn and is now somewhere else impressing another new client while replacements are in the process of taking residence and settling in their new home. This situation can be avoided by requiring the contractor to assign only persons to the contract who are expected to provide service from the beginning.

When use of transition teams is discouraged, personnel problems can be resolved at the start, and on-site indoctrination does not have to be repeated. It is also advisable that the client stipulate that all full-time security officers being assigned to a company be committed to work only at the facility for which they were hired. This requirement helps avoid assignment of security officers to work an 8-hour shift at one location after they have completed an 8-hour shift at another company. It also prevents the contractor from arbitrarily shifting a trained guard from one location to another client's facility.

TRANSMISSION OF STATEMENT OF WORK TO VENDOR

When the statement of work is completed, it should be sent via registered mail to each of the selected bidders together with a request for proposal. A specific time and date are established for return of bidders' proposals. Time extensions may be granted at the convenience of the client if there is a compelling reason to grant them to contractors who may not be able to complete a proposal in a timely manner for extenuating reasons. Extreme caution should be exercised to ensure that there can be no suggestion of unethical treatment, favoritism, or partiality in dealing with vendors. An extension given to one contractor should apply to all bidders.

SUMMARY

The value of a comprehensive statement of work is clear. It is the core document that defines each requirement, stipulation, standard, expectation, and regulation on which a quality service is to be provided. When a final, legally binding contract is executed between client and contractor, the statement of work becomes a part of that contract and has the full force and effect of the contract itself. It is useful when damages are alleged to have been suffered between the client and another party because of action or lack of action by a security guard or when litigation involves the contract guard force. If the client can show that it took all reasonable and prudent measures to protect life and property and has documented these measures in a comprehensive statement of work and other instructions to the contractor and that the contractor has failed to properly perform the requirements, the effects of litigation against the client may be mitigated to some degree depending on the circumstances in each situation.

6

Vendor Selection

The quality of security service being provided to a user company depends largely on how thoroughly the user searches and evaluates potential bidders for the service contract. For clients interested only in selecting the lowest-price bidder, it makes no difference which contractor is chosen because the clients obtain only what they pay for regardless of the provider. A systematic search identifies preferred contractors who have the technical and managerial competence to administer a full-service contract and be responsive to the needs of the client. Contract security officers usually come from the same personnel pool within a specific venue. Although some possess better qualifications and abilities, the local management of the guard provider makes the final difference between quality service and lack of service. The purpose of this chapter is to disclose how this search and evaluation are conducted, preferably by the security project team.

NATIONAL CONTRACTS

There has been a recent trend for large companies to replace their security officer services at all operating locations with a single contractor selected by the corporate headquarters. The thinking is that more control can be exercised over the vendor because of corporate national buying power. This thought is enhanced by the fact that the client can stipulate what it deems value-added and continuous improvement standards the contractor must demonstrate a willingness to implement. This single national contract concept may have some theoretical merit, but it often is not practical.

For example, use of a national security service contract often removes all control from the local facilities and places it within the unilateral authority of a home office organization that may or may not have a concept of the security requirements of local branch offices and facilities. It also discourages competition because the local corporate facilities cannot unilaterally terminate the contract and select another vendor if there is flawed performance that remains uncorrected. The only recourse is to appeal to the corporate home office that procured the national contract and state the complaint against the offending vendor. The local facility must depend on those authorities to resolve problems when they cannot be settled on the local level. This well-intended philosophy appears to be favorable to the client, but there are other forces that influence the results. Among these are that the contractor's local management realizes it is secure in a multiyear contract over which the facilities serviced within the jurisdiction have little control.

If the complaints are not widespread, the contractor might recognize that the client's corporate office is reluctant to cancel the contract on the basis of complaints from what may be a relatively small number of facilities. This changes only when a preponderance of facilities raise overwhelming objection to the services provided by the contractor over an extended period of time. Such compelling objections reflect adversely on the vendor's commitment to continuing improvement and providing value-added services. However, unless these elements are stated in clearly measurable terms and audited frequently, this commitment may be an illusory marketing device. Much attention may be given at the onset of the contract but may be relegated to lesser importance as the contract progresses.

Other than stipulating an adjustment in the payment of charges as a penalty for failed performance, one of the most drastic actions that can be taken against a nonperforming vendor is cancellation of the contract. Because the prerogative rests solely within the purview of the corporate office, managers often are unwilling to resort to such action because it can mean that their decision-making competencies and methods used to select a vendor might be challenged.

If a large corporation chooses to use a national contract, it should recognize that each individual office of the vendor has different types of managers; some are excellent, others are less so. That a corporate office may have outstanding success with one vendor at the parent location is no assurance that the same level of managerial performance is being made available to facilities at distant locations.

A company may consider nominating several preferred security vendors and permit local management to select one with which it negotiates its own contract for security services if desired. This encourages competition and provides the local business unit with at least nominal authority to direct the security program to best individual requirements. It also helps eliminate indifference on the part of the local vendor because the power to direct the contract now resides with the individual organization being serviced. As an added benefit, problems can be resolved more expeditiously than they can by an intermediary at a distant home office.

Consideration should be given to varying wages from one section of the country to another. Unless wages are negotiated in a single national contract, a local business unit may be able to negotiate a contract in which quality services are provided at a cost less than originally negotiated by a central purchasing authority in another geographic location.

VENDOR SELECTION

Regardless where or by whom a contractor is eventually selected, the most important consideration is the method by which the best qualified bidders are chosen and from whom proposals are solicited. This should be done on a local basis because actual management of the contract falls within the purview of the management of the local vendor. At the beginning of the selection process, individual management representatives of vendors undergo interviews during which they are expected to provide essential elements of information regarding their operations. The following areas should be examined closely.

Size of Vendor's Operation

It is important that the prospective client know the approximate size of the vendor's company. This indicates how much of the local market share of security business the company retains. If the vendor has a substantial portion of the business, it is an indicator that it has satisfied customers and is providing above-average service. Vendors should provide the number of hours of business per week they currently have and a list of their five largest accounts in the area. Large security contracts usually are provided to contractors who display high levels of technical proficiency. The list of clients may serve as a reference resource, but reference inquiries should not be limited to only the largest accounts.

Scope of Vendor's Management and Leadership

The scope of the vendor's management organization should be identified, because it is an indicator of management priorities in the service business. It also gives some measure of the leadership initiatives of the contractor. The vendor may be requested to provide a table of organization of on-site and off-site supervisory personnel to enable the client to determine the size and scope of the contractor's management and support teams.

Traditionally there have been distinct similarities in philosophies and structures of the security guard business and military-style organizations. There is a definite hierarchy in which the lower echelons must be effectively led and consistently motivated to complete a specific mission. The need for leadership is obvious, and a client should scrutinize the methods by which prospective bidders develop leaders within their organizations. Clients might question whether the contractor has a formal leadership training program, the manner in which potential leaders are identified, and the traits leaders must exhibit that differentiate them from others. It might be interesting to determine types of professional organizations in which prospective bidders hold membership and whether they participate in community activities.

It has been long believed that motivation must flow from the top down. Motivation should be stimulated from every direction. It is one of the factors for maintaining high morale among staff, encouraging personal pride, and overcoming indifference. In the operation of security officer forces, motivation usually comes from competent leaders, continuous training, responsive support, multilateral communication, and effective supervision. Motivation is instilled within the guard force by means of a systematic program of reward and recognition for achievement that requires a stretch of effort or other outstanding action or service. The client should carefully examine methods by which a prospective client encourages motivation within its guard staff. Examples of an effective motivational program include motivational and ethics training, internal newsletters, support services, awards programs, and supervisory activities.

The supervision provided to the guard staff is of exceptional importance. In most instances, an on-site supervisor is assigned for overall direction and administration of a medium to large guard force. This supervisor normally works a day shift in which he or she interacts frequently with the client's management. Shift leaders may be designated to maintain proper supervision during evening and midnight shifts in facilities where 24-hour coverage is needed. In smaller contracts, for which only one or two guards are assigned, supervision usually is provided by field supervisors who conduct inspections at frequent intervals normally determined by the client. Unannounced inspections performed on a periodic basis should be used as a training medium for security officers.

Vendor's Attrition Rate

The attrition rate within the prospective bidder's organization should be scrutinized. A generally high turnover rate for a high percentage of contracts may indicate poor management, lax supervision, or some other flaw in operation. A high rate of attrition may exist because the contractor consistently low-bids contracts to obtain business, and low wages are prevalent throughout the security officer force.

In determining the turnover rate, the client may use a bell curve that indicates the percentage of turnover at various wage levels. This may aid in identifying a problem within a bidder's operation that might be questioned. If the attrition rate appears remarkably high on certain shifts at one specific location, other factors may be involved and may be reasonably explained. For example, if the post is in an unsheltered, dimly lit location that requires the guard to patrol an expansive area alone and on foot at night, it may be difficult for the contractor to retain a minimum wage officer for such an adverse assignment, particularly during winter months. In many cases, the contractor may have no control over the condition if the user has rejected any attempts made by the contractor to alleviate the conditions. Lack of effort to solve the problem reflects the attitude that the contractor's management may not be responsive to the needs of its staff and may see a high attrition rate as an acceptable factor in doing business.

Vendor's Overtime Rate

The client may question the overtime percentage of the prospective bidder. Excessive overtime is an indicator of either a high turnover rate or a low staffing level. Both of these conditions can be considered negative factors that the client should discuss with the contractor's representative or with references.

Vendor's Training Commitment

The training a security officer receives is a matter discussed in various terms in several previous chapters. Because training is one of the most important considerations in the selection and maintenance of a competent security officer force, it is appropriate to address it further in the selection process for qualifying a bidder. Formal training before the assignment begins is expensive for a security vendor. Many contractors assert their commitment to providing trained guard personnel, but unless preassignment training is specified in the statement of work or mandated by state legislation, very little training is given and may not consist of much more than requiring a newly hired guard to watch training video tapes for several hours. This is not always the case in all situations. Some contractor organizations provide formal, multimedia educational programs for their guard personnel in a classroom environment. These have structured training programs conducted by experienced instructors. Although the methods and scope of training may vary, they reflect recognition of the value of providing personnel who have at least some perception of the tasks they are expected to perform.

During the selection interview, the user's representative may ask the contractor to provide information regarding actual classroom training given to the staff before assignment. It is appropriate to request that individual training records be submitted as proof of training. Some contractor's representatives may claim that the company complies with all training specifications mandated by state legislation. The client should be aware that in states that require security guard training, there are usually lengthy grace periods, as long as 120 days, in which the guard must undergo the specified training. This means a guard can be assigned to a user's facility for up to 4 months before he or she receives any training in basic responsibilities. The client should weigh carefully the value of a guard who has at least fundamental knowledge of the duties he or she is expected to perform against the cost of a guard who, before assignment as a security officer, may have driven a delivery truck all his or her working life.

Employment Practices

Some contractors claim that rather than conduct a formal training program, they hire only former or off-duty law enforcement officers, military personnel, or other classifications of workers who are expected to have all of the desired attributes of an exceptional security officer. This statement should sound strong alarm bells in the mind of the client's representative. It shows that many of the guard staff may be part-time workers. If they are off-duty police or military personnel, they cannot always be depended on to report for guard duty because of the unpredictable demands of their full-time employment, especially if a natural disaster occurs and they are needed for public emergency functions.

Many, if not most, jurisdictions stipulate that commissioned law enforcement officers be official agents of the state or municipality that employs them and that they retain their full police powers regardless of their duty status. In some political entities, police officers are expected to be armed even while off-duty. As law enforcement officers, they are obligated to do certain things, in a certain way, and in certain cases, particularly if a crime is committed in their presence. When such conditions and actions are sanctioned by law, the question becomes, at what point can law enforcement officers cease their obligations and capacity as public officers and defer to the less-demanding requirements of a private employer? A private security guard without arrest powers is not so constrained. They normally follow the policies and procedures associated with their assignment.

Under normal circumstances, the differences in the roles of police officer and private security guard are well defined. The boundary can become less distinct when the law enforcement officer also assumes the role of a private security guard and may raise serious questions in some jurisdictions. These questions and related liability matters are sensitive issues that should be resolved by legal counsel before off-duty police officers are assigned as security officers in a private facility. In many jurisdictions such employment is permitted, but clients are advised to determine the full legal ramifications of engaging in this activity within their areas before making any decisions of this nature.

Nature of Vendor's Accounts

The selection process should include examination of the type of accounts being retained by the potential bidder. The client should be aware that there are different types of contracts in which the bidder may be involved. Among these are annual contracts, in which a new bid is solicited each year and only the lowest bidder is selected. A contractor would find it difficult consistently to be a low bidder in these cases, and loss of these contracts is not necessarily due to poor performance.

Multiyear contracts are usually for a 3-year period with options to renew at 1-year intervals. These may or may not require the contract to be awarded to the lowest bidder. If the client exercises flexibility in the award process and bases the award on a composite scale according to the management, technical, and financial proposals, loss of this type of contract may reflect dissatisfaction with the incumbent contractor's performance and should be investigated through reference discussion with the former client.

Open-ended contracts, also known as *evergreen contracts* in some areas, are contracts let and automatically renewed on an annual basis as long as the client is satisfied with the services and billing rates are provided. Termination of an open-ended contract is usually caused by degradation in service or escalation of billing rates to an unacceptable level. When considering an open-ended contract, the user must assume that the billing rates naturally increase each year to maintain parity with wages at other locations and to ensure stability and quality within the guard force. At some point, these contracts have to be re-bid, or the user chooses to hire its own guards.

Vendor's Overhead Costs

Overhead costs vary within security contractors according to the management support provided by the contractor. Higher-quality contractors operating with higher-quality clients usually have higher overhead costs. In some instances costs are generally consistent among contractors. One example is general liability rates. The client should be careful to note and examine several percentage points' variance between contractors. During the prequalification phase, a wise client questions the reasons for a general liability rate that appears higher than others. The cause may be an unusually high job-related injury rate, which has an adverse influence on selection of a contractor.

Vendor's Employee Benefits

During the prequalification process, the client should examine whether the potential contractor offers benefits to its employees. Benefits generally are provided to the guard force only when the client is willing to pay for them. Some companies offer a minimum benefit policy to all employees, and it is important that the client know the cost of the policy. If the statement of work stipulates that a specific amount for benefits is priced into the billing rate, the cost of the free minimal benefits being paid by the contractor should be deducted. For example, if all a security contractor's employees are provided with 9 cents of benefits for each hour worked, and the client agrees to pay 75 cents per hour for benefits, the charge to the client should be only 66 cents per hour, because the contractor is already paying 9 cents of this amount to all of its employees. This applies to cost plus fixed overhead and profit but should not apply to cost plus management fees. In some cases, clients pay monthly for benefits, such as health insurance, that an employee receives during the month.

INVESTIGATION OF VENDOR

A client that uses the approach of carefully scrutinizing the qualifications of a potential bidder is better prepared to avoid routinely quoted rates and to eliminate the few bidders who may be obviously unqualified to perform a quality, value-added service. Focus should be directed at contractors who have reflected professional business knowledge and strategies and are agreeable to providing security service consistent with the requirements of the client. At this point, the client may reduce the number of bidders to those to be seriously considered as finalists in the bidding process.

The following phase of contractor preselection consists of investigating the financial status and background of each finalist organization by means of a business investigation report and inquiries made of former and existing clients. Other information regarding contractors can be obtained from computerized services such as Nexus and Lexus to determine whether the company had been involved in litigation or other noteworthy activities that may be of interest to the client. It is preferred that inquiries made to other clients of the contractor be made personally by telephone. Conflicting information can be discussed more freely this way than when adverse comments are committed to writing, as in a formal questionnaire. The following are questions that might be asked of a reference:

1. Type of contract
2. Size of contract in terms of staffing
3. Number of posts
4. Guard quality
5. Supervisory quality
6. Management support and liaison with user management
7. Billing accuracy
8. Performance standards
9. Attrition rate
10. Safety records
11. Guard appearance and attitudes
12. Scheduling and overtime
13. Compliance with statement of work

The information learned from discussions with references and other background data further assists clients in assigning weighted factors to the overall evaluation of bidders and helps them move closer to intelligent selection of a successful vendor.

REQUESTS FOR PROPOSAL

Requests for proposal and statements of work should be sent to each of the selected bidders. These documents should stipulate a firm response date and time. The user firm may include a statement in the request for proposal that explains to the contractor the methods by which the client evaluates each proposal. A sample description may include the following:

1. The purpose of the evaluation
2. The manner in which the proposal is to be formatted, that is, management, technical, and financial sections
3. The weight factors to be placed on each section
4. How bidders' management and technical sections are ranked, that is, most favorable to least favorable before consideration of cost
5. How the price proposals are ranked, that is, highest to lowest
6. Bidder's understanding of the statement of work
7. Bidder's response to mandatory items and implementation plans
8. Bidder's quality control and management leadership programs
9. Bidder's performance history on similar contracts
10. Determination of the bidder who best suits the needs of the client

Contractors whose bids are eliminated should be notified that their initial responses were deemed not consistent with the objectives of the client and that no formal proposals will be solicited from them at this time. If the client chooses, the unsuccessful bidders may be given an opportunity to request a debriefing regarding the reasons they were not selected as the winning contractor.

SUMMARY

The search for a quality vendor to bring value to the client is an arduous and complex process that requires much research. This chapter reviews the benefits of contracting for security services on the local level as opposed to use of national contracts. Further discussion addresses the requirements associated with an in-depth look at a contractor's operation, its management, leadership commitments, history of performance, and other elements associated with a contractor organization that is successful above all others. The success of a contractor in many ways is expected to contribute to a successful security relationship with the client's company.

7

Proposal Evaluation

Having completed the statement of work and a request for proposal, the security project team can begin evaluating the responses from the selected contractors and decide which provider is best qualified to provide the services that best suit the requirements of the organization. This is a systematic process that requires application of logical and analytical thought. This chapter is intended to aid the team in its efforts by working through assessment of the various sections of a proposal to reach an informed decision. The information contained herein may aid a contractor in developing a definitive proposal.

MAKING A DIFFERENCE

Many years of experience preparing statements of work and evaluating security-related proposals have shown me that security contractors' proposals come in all shapes and sizes. Some are nothing more than a single sheet of paper containing little more than price information. Others are professional-appearing and include color advertising brochures, technical qualifications, management biographies, financial data, and an impressive list of prestigious clients. The common element in these two types of proposals is that neither of them responds to the specific requirements defined in the statement of work.

In some instances, contractors may add the simple statement that they understand and comply with the statement of work; however, there have been times when it is obvious in these proposals that the contractor has either not read that document or is totally indifferent to its contents. The contractor's advertising brochures may assert that they are better than all others, but the contractor expects potential clients to take a leap of faith that what is being said is true.

Then there are the high-quality proposals that are totally responsive to the statement of work and define precisely the contractor's understanding of the tasks to be performed and identify how the services blend with the culture of the client and support the client's asset-protection objectives. The result is that the proposal is the most important mechanism that gives contractors the opportunity to prove how they are better than others.

Preparing a proposal takes time, effort, and creativity on the part of the bidder. It is not a matter of merely developing rates and adding some off-the-shelf boilerplate material to provide volume to the proposal. The contractor should carefully examine the client's statement of work and address every point in detail to explain precisely how the contractor intends to implement each requirement. By responding to each issue in the statement of work, contractors demonstrate their commitment to be responsive to all interests of the client. Using this approach, contractors can define their management techniques, explain their supervisory strategies, prove their technical expertise, and give impetus to their own initiatives to satisfy the client. It allows them a platform from which they might launch new ideas beneficial to the client. In this manner, the contractor is providing a cogent proposal that contains facts and information measurable and capable of being given weight and substance by the client.

Some contractors define their managerial capabilities and their technical competencies in a single section to provide a degree of cohesiveness to their proposals. Although these areas may be combined this way, they are better defined separately in the same section. If the security project team approach has been used, the team might be evaluating the management and the technical sections of the contractor's proposal. If the team concept has not been used, however, some sections of the proposal might be evaluated by persons with the most intimate knowledge of the firm's security requirements and other sections by those whose main interest is not necessarily the protection of the company's assets. It is essential that those evaluating the proposals be able to compare the company's expectations from a security provider with the vendor's description of how it intends to achieve the objectives. Persons with only superficial knowledge of the company's security requirement cannot make a valid interpretation.

Proposals should be addressed to an impartial management official excluded from the proposal evaluation process. The management and technical sections are given to the evaluating authorities, and the financial section should be sealed and retained by this official until all other sections have been assessed. The purpose is to allow objective evaluation of the quality of management and technical capabilities of each vendor without being influenced by cost. For example, a bidder may project the lowest cost but may lack the professional competence and resources to effectively perform the contract requirements. The objective is to establish the level of technical competence of each bidder to satisfy the client's objectives before costs are considered.

It is suggested that the evaluating team devise a numerical weighting system to be assigned to the review of each section of the proposals. Because the priorities of each organization differ, any rating system should give serious consideration to the values of greatest importance to the organization. These are listed in order of precedence, most important to least important. The evaluating team should be aware that intangible values may be written in the proposal that might differentiate a particular vendor from others and benefit the client. An example might be a suggestion from a vendor regarding the manner in which communication between the contractor and client would be enhanced over and above the methods stipulated in the statement of work. These values should be given appropriate weight in the proposal evaluation.

CONTRACTOR MANAGEMENT PLAN

The contractor's management plan is usually given first consideration. In this section, the vendor is expected to describe its organization and overall management concepts. It identifies the names and backgrounds of the principal manager and supervisory personnel and discloses each of their responsibilities. The plan should include organizational and functional charts that reflect lines of authority and reporting. If the vendor is the local office of a large national security organization, the relation between the two entities should be explained in terms of home office support, corporate direction, corporate assessments, and other association.

This section provides the opportunity for the vendor to detail its leadership strategies and define its leadership development programs. The contractor may use this opportunity to describe how its quality assurance programs are established and give specific examples of the success of this effort. If the contractor's organization has advanced management training programs, these may be described in measurable terms for the client's review. Other training and educational programs for other levels of personnel may be identified. The contractor should describe experience with similar clients and describe any awards, commendations, and other accomplishments achieved that differentiate the contractor as a premier organization.

The management section of the proposal should include the contractor's definition of how it plans to implement the overall supervision of the contract. The vendor must be innovative in describing this plan. It should not merely play back the stipulations in the statement of work to the client but use ingenuity in prescribing management methods that achieve the results desired by the client while establishing a client-vendor relationship that meets the changing security objectives.

The contractor should define its commitment to continuous improvement and provide examples of successes in this effort. A wise contractor relates these examples to the objectives of the client and identifies how they can be either integrated with the client's goals or at least be harmonious with them. The management section should be used as the medium by which the contractor describes how it will maintain liaison with the client's management and be responsive to changing requirements. Although the management section of a proposal may not carry the same weight factors as the financial portion, it should be a strong statement of the vendor's management capabilities, because that is what the client is paying for.

The technical portion of the contractor's management plan in the proposal identifies the contractor's ability to perform the operational aspects of the contract. This is a broad-based section that defines in detail the vendor's understanding of each requirement for each post on each shift. These should be explained by the client providing the job descriptions in the statement of work. This portion of the proposal might define the contractor's understanding and performance of training requirements, inspection and supervisory functions, personnel support, records and reports, recruiting and screening methods, physical and mental qualifications of each assignee, and all other operational stipulations in the statement of work. The contractor's response should be in an order that corresponds to each mandatory requirement as it appears in the statement of work. This facilitates evaluation to maintain continuity and expedite the orderly assessment of each item.

CONTRACTOR'S UNDERSTANDING OF THE SCOPE OF WORK

As with the management portion of a proposal, it is unacceptable that the bidder respond with a blanket statement that it "understands and will comply with the statement of work." Such a statement does not give the evaluating authorities any tangible or measurable information or evidence on which the proposal may be evaluated in comparison with others. This statement should send the message to the evaluators that the vendor agrees to anything to obtain a contract but afterward conducts business as usual. Contractors who do not make an effective response to a statement of work in their proposals are in jeopardy of embarrassing themselves if a client asks for an oral presentation after submission of a proposal. Contractors must be able to justify how the contract is to be administered by answering questions put to them by an evaluation board. This option usually is exercised in the award of national or larger contracts, but it remains an option for any company outsourcing a security service.

The technical portion of the management plan offers the contractor another opportunity to identify its strengths and to develop a deeper association with a client that drives value into the relationship. By using creativity, ingenuity, and a deep understanding of the customer, a contractor may be able to identify areas within the client's structure in which the security contractor might be able to offer certain technology it possesses or other services associated with the security concerns of the client organization but not specifically identified in the statement of work. When such an offer is made, the contractor should clearly identify the manner in which these services support or enhance the specific interests of the client. If unsolicited contributions are included in the contractor's proposal, the evaluation team should explore them to determine whether the proposed services have feasibility or applicability to any other company initiatives. If they are found to have value, the contributions should add weight to the proposal. If the offerings have no immediate or foreseeable value to the company, the contractor should at least be given credit for the initiative.

Vendors should state whether subcontractors are to be employed on any part of the contract to perform work the vendor is unable to achieve for technical or cost reasons. The client retains the prerogative to examine subcontractors' proposals and to accept or reject those proposals. When used, subcontractors should be held to the same standards of performance and cost as stipulated for the original vendor in the statement of work.

The contractor should include information regarding compliance with insurance requirements, such as employers liability and occupational disease liability, comprehensive general liability, comprehensive automobile liability, fidelity insurance, false arrest insurance, and other requirements stipulated by the client. The vendor should address requirements concerning operating licenses, handgun licenses if necessary, compliance with state-mandated training for security officers where applicable, and other technical certificates or other legal demands made by the client or by local, state, or federal law.

ADDRESSING TRAINING

When a contractor provides advanced training to the guard force that exceeds that mandated by state law or by the statement of work, the nature and extent of the training should be defined as a positive statement for consideration when the proposal is evaluated. When the training specifications in a statement of work are less than is routinely provided by the bidder, the contractor should not take this to mean that guards receiving less-than-normal training may be assigned to the contract. The contractor should use this requirement as a means to actively demonstrate to the client just how rigorously they do train newly assigned personnel. The contractor also should use this portion of the proposal to keep the client's attention focused on tasks the vendor is capable of performing and to describe its use of innovation to achieve quality results in complying with the statement of work. The contractor must describe in detail how it can perform stellar service and why the client should choose it as a successful bidder. It is impossible for bidders to receive credit for things they keep secret.

By studying each proposal on a point-for-point basis and assigning the predetermined weight factors to them, the evaluation team can rank the contractor's management proposals. At this point, the team can identify the leading bidders and narrow the selection process to several contractors.

COST PROPOSAL

The team now begins evaluation of the cost proposal. Elements should be considered in review of the financial proposal that may save the client money and of which the evaluating authorities should be aware. These represent some of the techniques in which a contractor may acquire additional profits during the life of the contract that are not specified in the financial and cost section. They are commonly known as *drop profits*.

On the surface, drop profits represent small amounts of money that the client may not notice. When continued over time, however, they can accrue to relatively large sums. These techniques are not illegal and are not practiced by many security service companies. There are a few, however, who might exploit an opportunity to add drop profits to their billing if the client is unaware that these practices are occurring. Some security service companies may describe questionable concepts regarding their cost of doing business, as follows:

1. Overhead costs that increase substantially on an annual basis. Certain overhead costs increase as they do in any business in which there is growth. Management wages are probably the most notable of these, and insurance costs and payroll taxes may be others. However, management and supervisory salaries are often prorated among the accounts, and a percentage is charged back to the clients. Many administrative overhead costs, such as supplies, advertising, stock uniforms, equipment, and similar expenses generally do not fluctuate widely and can usually be projected on a yearly basis. Office space, communication, vehicles, and office equipment leases frequently are fixed on a long-term basis and remain the same for several years. The most obvious cause of increased overhead expenses may be a reduction in the contractor's client base.

2. New contract start-up costs increase overhead and management expenses. This concept might be partly correct if the contractor is forced to lease new office space and employ management and supervisory personnel to administer the contract above those identified in the statement of work. Because this is rarely the case in small contracts (those less than 1000 hours per week of service), the contractor's overhead is already being paid by the various existing accounts. A portion of any additional overhead charges consequently can be considered profit over the amount factored into the billing rate; it therefore becomes drop profit.

A client may realize further savings by scrutinizing benefits and vacation billing rates. Insurance benefits and vacation allowances are given to full-time employees only. In most cases, a 90-day employment period is required before insurance benefits become effective. An employee also is not usually entitled to paid vacation until after 1 year of continued employment. There are instances in which these charges appear with the first billing, regardless of the status of the assigned personnel unless otherwise directed in the statement of work. The following is a further example of cost savings by means of closely examining benefits and vacation billing charges.

Certain assumptions must be considered. The first concerns the fact that for around-the-clock service, 168 hours are needed to staff one post. For computation purposes, it is assumed that ten full-time posts are to be staffed. Because three shifts are needed for around-the-clock coverage on each post, three full-time and three part-time guards are used to fill this increment. The reader may question whether it is more prudent to use four full-time and one part-time security officers to fill the required posts. Sources who are managers and executives of contract security companies advise that they prefer to keep full-time personnel to a minimum and use part-time employees to a broader extent for cost and control purposes.

The second assumption concerns the basic billing structure for wages and benefits. This is as follows:

Basic Billing Structure

Hours per week	1680
Insurance benefits	$1.50 per hour
Vacation accrual	40 hours per year
Average hourly wage	$7.50 per hour

These figures are used for the following computations.

Vacation Rates for Full-time Staff

1680 hours ÷ 40 hours = 42 staff members
42 staff × 40 hours × $7.50 = $12,600.00
$12,600 + 15% payroll tax = $14,490.00
$14,490.00 ÷ 87,600 hours per year = 0.165 cents per billing hour

Insurance Rates for Full-time Staff

1680 staff hours @ $1.50 allowable benefits per week computed on an annual
    basis of 87,600 hours per year × $1.50 = $131,400.00 per year

If full-time guards perform 120 hours of service each week, the remaining 48 hours are filled by part-time guards not entitled to benefits. With this concept, the following additional profit to a vendor can be shown if the client is billed benefit rates for ineligible personnel:

48 hours × 10 posts ÷ 7 days × 365 days per year =
    25,029 hours per year × $1.50 = $43,543.50

Additional drop profits may be made by a contractor who bills a client for benefits ostensibly paid to newly assigned personnel who may not be eligible for benefits until after 90 days of employment. Using the assumption that the contract needs 30 full-time personnel at the start of the contract, the following computation is made:

8 hours per day × 30 staff × 90 days = 21,600 staff hours × $1.50 benefits =
    $32,400.00 additional profit

In this sample case, when the profits from the payments made from these ineligible benefits are combined, the contractor may obtain a total of $75,943.50 drop profit.

A contractor may use other forms of actions to obtain small amounts of drop profit. One example is that a full-time guard may be suspended from one or more days of vacation as a disciplinary measure for an infraction. Because the client has paid toward this accrual, the contractor may retain this payment because it has been forfeited by the guard. Although this amount is usually quite small, it might accrue to one of some importance if this practice is spread throughout the contractor's client base and is used frequently. In similar cases, the client contributes to the vacation accrual because a guard may terminate employment before the one-year anniversary date. This accrual may be retained by the contractor rather than paid to the guard at the time of separation.

It should be reemphasized that these may be isolated cases and that not all security service contractors engage in these unethical practices, but the evaluation team should be aware of such tactics to properly appraise each proposal. There should be no hesitancy on the part of the client to allow a reasonable profit to the vendor if they are to expect high-quality managerial and personnel support. However, contractors should be straightforward in their cost proposals and be required to justify each expense and billing rate. The client should stipulate in the statement of work that all vacation pay, medical insurance, and other benefits should be billed only as the legitimate cost is incurred.

The security project team should examine any costs related to equipment to be provided by the vendor. These include items such as patrol vehicles, two-way radio communication, special protective equipment, firearms, and any other nature of item specified in the statement of work. These costs are usually absorbed by the client with the cost of any maintenance insurance agreements and are usually amortized over a three-year period.

If vehicles are to be provided by the contractor, the client should inform the vendor of the manufacture and model of the preferred vehicle and the number of daily miles the vehicle is expected to travel to allow the bidder to project costs for fuel and maintenance unless the client is willing to provide fuel for the vehicle. The recommended maintenance schedule of new vehicles aids vendor and client in projecting maintenance costs over the life of the contract. Costs for cleaning and repairs of the vehicle rest with the contractor, but the client should be aware that its employees may not operate the vehicle for any reason. Equipment costs for vehicles should be invoiced monthly and include the following line items:

1. Amortized monthly cost
2. Monthly insurance costs
3. Fuel cost
4. Prorated cost for routine maintenance schedule

If the client provides a patrol vehicle for the security guards to use for patrol work, the vendor should be required to name the user as additional insured on the contractor's comprehensive general liability policy and agree to provide motor vehicle insurance when the contractor's employees are operating the vehicle. When a client provides equipment for the contractor, the client assumes general responsibility for repairs, fuel, and maintenance. These costs can often be quite high because of the nature of a security patrol in which the patrol car is usually driven at relatively slow speeds for short periods of time. In this case, the client is responsible for the cost of the vehicle, registration, licensing, and insurance. In certain cases, particularly when the client may have a fleet of leased vehicles, it may appear superficially less expensive for the client to provide vehicles to the contractor, but when these expenses are added to the overall cost of the guard service contract, they may exceed those for a vehicle provided and maintained by the contractor.

The bidder should provide detailed cost data for all expense items with figures to one-tenth cents, e.g., $8.378, so that the client may round the figures or retain them as presented, whichever may be to their advantage. The evaluation team should not accept a financial proposal that includes only a summary of cost data and does not provide a detailed description of all expenses as they are applied over the life of the contract.

The security project team should make careful notes regarding any questions that may arise during the proposal appraisal process. These may be documented and returned to the remaining individual bidders for resolution with a request to submit a best and final cost offer. Some companies find an advantage in holding individual pre-award meetings with the contractors. In these meetings the vendor may give an oral presentation regarding its ability to administer and manage the contract, especially when the statement of work is complex or contains highly differentiated requirements.

Selected members of the security project team should visit the contractor's local offices and obtain a first-hand view of the administrative operation, including hiring procedures, record keeping, classroom training, and similar activities. Such a visit, particularly if it is unannounced, can be extremely enlightening in evaluating the contractor's ability to provide service.

AWARDING THE CONTRACT

After completion of the proposal evaluation and application of the selected form of measurement to every segment of each proposal, the team is in a position to place the proposals in an order that ranks them from the most acceptable to the least acceptable contractor. At this point, the client should be ready to award a contract. The unsuccessful vendors should be notified of the client's decision at the same time as the successful bidder is advised of the award. It is not appropriate that any information regarding the award of the contract become known to any outside source before release of the final award notification. The client should apply every degree of propriety and ethics in making the evaluation to avoid any accusation of favoritism or partiality and, if the user is a public agency, to defend its decision if a protest is filed.

SUMMARY

Selection of a security service contractor is usually based on critical examination of proposals submitted by bidders. This requires comprehensive assessment of each part of the proposal to determine its relevance to the requirements stipulated in the statement of work. This chapter attempts to aid the project security team in going through that process by examining the elements of a proposal to reach a successful conclusion. A decided advantage of conducting a thorough proposal evaluation is that the client becomes intimately familiar with the successful contractor's operation and by the time selection is made develops the beginnings of a strong relationship with several of the contractor's managers.

8

Monitoring a Contract

As stated earlier, most things naturally evolve downward unless they are supported and given attention during their lifetime. The same may be said of a service contract. The award of a security services contract is not the end of the process but the beginning of a new one. That is, monitoring the contract to ensure that the selected provider adheres to the stipulations of the agreement and that the quality of service promised is produced. This chapter addresses the requirement for monitoring the contract by client and contractor to ensure the goal is reached.

WHY MONITOR A CONTRACT?

Some companies use the services of a security contractor and trust that the service is managed effectively without any supervision on the client's part. An example of this thinking involves a midwestern company that for more than 14 years had retained the same contractor to provide security officers at its facility. Each year, the contract was renewed by means of issuance of a purchase order that accommodated the annual increase in the cost of the service. Over the years, the contractor's management changed many times, and the company itself had gone through three acquisitions. The client had gone through various managerial upheavals, but the security service contract chugged along unchanged. At no time during those years had the original contract been reviewed or had the contract been renegotiated or rebid. The client recognized the security service was merely mediocre, but nothing was done to assess the service, billing, or any other facet of the operation to determine whether the client was receiving the quality of service for which it was paying. That was left entirely to the contractor's management, because, in the client's opinion, this is what it was paying for. This was truly an evergreen contract.

With appointment of a new security manager in the client's company, a review was finally made of the contractor's services. It was discovered that although the cost of service increased annually, the security officers' wages had remained unchanged for years at a time. The client also was being charged a rate, including benefits, for all full-time officers when less than one half of them actually worked full time. Supervision and training were almost nonexistent, as was communication between the contractor's and the client's management. Although the client expected that contractor to provide a minimum of 16 hours of preassignment training, it was learned that many of the guards received no training at all, with the exception of the instructions to new security officers regarding how to find the client's location.

It was clear that the contract had deteriorated beyond the point of resurrection. It was equally obvious that for years the client had been paying for services it assumed it was receiving but did not. Whether this was due to unethical practices on the part of the contractor or indifference to the contract on the part of both parties will never be known. What is known is that the contract was recompeted, and a careful contract monitoring process was established to ensure no repetition of past practices.

One can only wonder whether other companies use contractor security services and may be having similar experiences without realizing it. The answer can be found with continuous and careful monitoring of contract services and holding the contractor to a mutually agreed level of quality performance.

SELECTING THE CONTRACT MONITOR

In almost every case, the customer must take a proactive stance in monitoring postaward performance of the contract and managing the outsourced relationship if it is to retain control of the relationship and ensure that it receives the maximum value the outsourcing relationship offers. This may necessitate that a client dedicate a competent person who has the explicit goal of monitoring performance of the contract and managing and extracting value from the relationship. This person is known as the *contract monitor* and should be identified to the contractor as being the person with responsibility of representing the client in all contractual matters.

Strong consideration should be given to selection of this person and the position he or she should hold in the organization. In many cases, the contract security officer force is regarded as a supplement to the company's security department. In other instances, the guard force comes under the jurisdiction of a maintenance department or human relations department or other type of support organization. The manager of the department to which the security guard force reports most probably insists on being the primary point of contact between the company and the guard force vendor. This is only logical, because there must be a direct link between the guard force and the organization to which it is responsible.

Depending on the size of the contract, monitoring of all facets of its performance can be time consuming. Unless the department to which the security service reports has the staff available either full time or part time to perform the contract-monitoring function, the company has to consider adding to that staff or assigning the task elsewhere within the organization. If it is to be reassigned, there has to be an understanding about which person becomes the primary point of contact with the vendor's management and who else has the authority to mandate contract changes, adjust costs, and resolve other administrative, operational, and financial issues.

This problem typically is solved by assigning monitoring of the overall contract to the security manager and performing financial audits to the business management department or similar internal organization. Regardless of how contract monitoring is assigned, the person or persons with the responsibility must possess sufficient stature and authority to cross internal organizational boundaries and command support from the various departments within the company. They must have sole authority for making contractual changes, issuing task orders, levying penalties, and generally representing the company in all aspects of monitoring the contract.

MONITORING VERSUS MANAGING

A distinction should be made between managing a contract and monitoring it. A client may believe it is obliged to manage the contract as it relates to business operations. However, the client should not attempt to manage the infrastructure of the contractor or direct or supervise contract employees. Doing so may create a situation in which the contractor employees can be regarded as secondary employees and cause the client to become a co-employer of the contract personnel and cause conflicts. Client and contractor are two separate companies.

The main obligation of a client is to monitor the activities of the contractor to ensure that all stipulations of the contract are being fulfilled in a satisfactory manner. This includes elements such as frequent assessment of contractor employees' performance, billing accuracy, responsiveness of contractor management, attrition, training, and other matters that have a bearing on the overall performance of the contract. Direction of the vendor's employees is a function the vendor's management is being paid to achieve. It is within the vendor's sole province to accomplish this task in accordance with the contractual stipulations and subject to enforcement by the client's representative.

GETTING UP CLOSE AND PERSONAL

The local management of the contractor has the responsibility for "getting up close and personal" with the client by establishing bilateral and harmonious lines of communication between them. This task should not rest only with the contractor's on-site supervisor. Unquestionably, the on-site supervisor must have daily contact with the client's representative to discuss day-to-day operations, but this in itself is insufficient for overall management of the contract. It is imperative that the security service manager schedule meetings with the client's management to review all contractual security activity and any anticipated changes in the user's business that might necessitate involvement by the vendor. The vendor must take the initiative to approach the client with an agenda on a frequent and regular basis before problems arise. In these meetings, the contractor has the opportunity to discuss quality-control strategies, staffing, problem-solving techniques, and other pertinent activities. This can be an appropriate occasion for the contractor to make the client aware of new technologies or services it may have to offer and to examine methods to improve the relationship.

MONITORING SERVICE COMPLAINTS

The responsibilities of the contract monitor include a wide range of activities, one of which is investigation of complaints concerning the security officer force. These allegations must be resolved expeditiously to maintain credibility within the security organization. The contract monitor should document each complaint and make inquiries as necessary to confirm or refute the allegation. In many cases, these complaints involve minor situations, such as rudeness to an employee, and can be solved by merely interviewing the parties involved. If the offense proves to be factual, the contract monitor can request that the on-site supervisor counsel the officer responsible or take other disciplinary action in accordance with the contractor's policies. The contract monitor should take no direct disciplinary measure against a contractor employee.

In a similar sense, security officers may file a complaint against an employee who fails to follow security procedures. In this case, the contract monitor discusses the matter with the employee's supervisor to ensure that the violator understands and adheres to security policies. Such intercession should educate employees to the roles and responsibilities of the security officers and to their own security obligations to the welfare of the company. The knowledge that the security officer force has the support of company management reduces potential risk for further confrontations between officers and employees. When a complaint has been resolved, the contract monitor should advise the complainant, preferably in writing, with regard to the actions taken.

In some situations serious allegations may be made against a contractor employee that necessitate more extensive investigation. Depending on the circumstances of the complaint, the contract monitor has the authority to direct the contractor to conduct an internal investigation at no expense to the client to resolve the issue. In such cases, the contractor management has to become involved. The results of the investigation must be made known to the contract monitor as should any definitive actions on the part of the contractor that are acceptable to the client.

MONITORING TRAINING REQUIREMENTS

Other contractual matters that require substantial attention by the contract monitor involve the contractor's maintenance of training and qualification specifications for assigned personnel. Although the service provider agrees to comply with these stipulations when the contract is executed, there is usually some slippage in the fulfillment of these obligations as the contract progresses. Unless the guard force is unusually stable with little or no attrition, there is some turnover in the guard staff. When vacancies are filled with new hires, there is potential for untrained employees to be placed within a client's facility, often in the expectation that the new employee will receive sufficient on-the-job training to enable them to perform with at least minimal effectiveness. When the contract requires a specified number of preassignment training hours, the contract monitor may require that the vendor provide training records for each employee being assigned to the facility as assurance that the individual meets the minimal qualifications and training requirements. A duplicate set of training records should be required at the client's site, where they can be readily available for periodic inspection by the contract monitor. If there are repeated occasions when unqualified employees are assigned to the user's organization and the contractor does not respond to the deficiency in a satisfactory manner, the contract monitor may resort to compensation adjustment as a penalty to the vendor.

The extent of on-the-job training must be monitored. As with other things, the effectiveness of on-the-job training has a tendency to evolve downward unless it is frequently upheld and maintained to achieve the objectives for which it is intended. For example, if a perimeter gate is required to be closed at 8:00 P.M. and reopened at 8:00 A.M. each day, the original security officers may follow this routine precisely. As a succession of new officers are trained, the opening and closing times might begin to vary according to the perceptions and priorities of the different trainers. Over time, the gates may not be closed at all and expose the facility to serious risk and vulnerability. The client should specify the number of hours newly assigned security officers must work under direct supervision before they are permitted to work alone.

PERFORMING AUDITS AND INSPECTIONS

The contract monitor should perform periodic audits of each post on selected shifts, some of which have to be performed during closed hours. These audits allow the contract monitor to evaluate the performance of the guards and determine how the tasks are being accomplished, compared with the methods prescribed for them to be achieved. The audit allows the contract monitor to discern which tasks are not being performed and to identify which guards need additional training or familiarization with standing policies and procedures.

In the performance of the audit, the contract monitor should examine all post and shift orders, the on-site supervisors' log books, training records, equipment and maintenance records, alarm response and incident reports, and all other documentation associated with the security officer force to ensure that all policies and procedures are current. When the audit is being performed, the contract monitor should be accompanied by a member of the contractor's management. The presence of the contractor's managers gives meaning to the audit in the eyes of the security officers and enhances the relationship with the contractor by permitting its participation in this function.

The audit should include examination and inventory of all client-furnished equipment. Unusual expenses, particularly for items such as flashlight batteries, automobile flares, first-aid supplies, and other disposable material, may indicate that these items are being misappropriated for security officers' personal use. Telephone costs should be examined to prevent unauthorized use or abuse of the client's telephone system by the guard force. If the client provides a patrol vehicle for the guard force, mileage records should be examined daily. In one case, a security manager noticed excessive mileage on a patrol car during a shift when the vehicle would normally be used the least. Investigation disclosed that the night-shift security officer supervisor was using the patrol car to drive home for dinner each evening. The results of the audit should be discussed in detail with the on-site supervisor and with the contractor's management. Remedial measures should be clearly stated and the client's expectations articulated to the vendor's supervisory personnel for action and response.

INSPECTING RECORDS AND REPORTS

Records and reports prepared by the individual guards are valuable tools for the contract monitor. By reviewing all shift and post reports on a daily basis, the monitor develops a clear picture of the activities that occur within the facility at all hours of the day, some of which may be of great interest to the security organization. These reports provide information about the performance of the individual guards. For example, if a guard post is known to be relatively active during a specified shift, and the guard on duty consistently reports that nothing unusual occurs, this may indicate the guard is inattentive to his or her duties or lacks common curiosity about the things around him or her. In this case, the contract monitor may suggest that the on-site supervisor observe the guard to determine the actual level of activity at the post or assign another guard at the post and compare reports. If the new guard describes situations and circumstances that should have been observed by the previous guard, a supervisory problem has emerged that warrants investigation and action by the on-site supervisor.

If a noted hazard does not require immediate attention, the guard reports identify fire and safety hazards and maintenance problems, which the contract monitor forwards to the respective departments for correction. If safety, security, and maintenance deficiencies are repeatedly reported by the guards and there is no evidence of any action being taken to correct them, the contract monitor should intercede with the managers of the department concerned to determine whether there is a reason no remedial action has been taken. If there is a valid reason for the inactivity, the guards should be advised of this reason.

SUPPORTING THE CONTRACTOR EMPLOYEES

One of the most common complaints from a guard force is that the client's management frequently takes no action on many of the matters reported to them. This sends the guards the demoralizing message that their efforts are not recognized and that no one pays attention to the many reports they are required to submit to the customer. A simple matter of a burned-out light bulb that is not replaced in a stairway may not be considered a matter of immediate importance to the user's maintenance manager, but it can be important to the safety of the security guard who must walk the darkened stairway at night. The contract monitor must be cognizant of contract performance and exercise authority to take the action necessary to support the contractor's employees and establish an environment in which they can effectively perform the tasks they were employed to accomplish.

MONITORING BILLING RATES

Billing rates and time records must receive prompt examination and all inconsistencies promptly referred to the attention of the contractor's management for resolution. Billing inaccuracies may be frequent when a large number of part-time personnel work erratic schedules or when the client requires additional guard staff on special occasions. The on-site supervisor typically prepares the time records of the guard staff and submits them to the contractor's billing department, where the figures may or may not be reviewed for accuracy. If billing errors are not detected and resolved immediately, they perpetuate and gradually worsen until the time comes when it becomes almost impossible to resolve them.

Chapter 7 discusses some of the more insidious methods by which additional costs might be charged to clients without their knowledge. Included in these tactics is the issue of *ghosting hours* whereby unethical contractors bill a client for hours that were never worked. For example, if one security officer calls off sick, no replacement is made either through substitution or a temporary officer, and the client is still billed as though the work occurred. Unless the contract monitor carefully examines each item on each billing statement and resolves every inconsistency, the anticipated cost savings by outsourcing the guard force may have less than meaningful consequences.

SUMMARY

When an outsourced security service fails to produce the desired results, it is typically attributable to one of two main factors, the performance of the guard service was not properly managed by the vendor or the relationship with the vendor was not properly managed by the client. A link between these problems may be a lack of bilateral communication compounded by misperceptions of what is expected from the service being contracted. In either case, clients must take control of the outsourced relationship by stating their expectations in specific and lucid terms to the contractor at the onset of the relationship with meaningful consequences attached. It is erroneous to relinquish control of a contract to a vendor and assume that the vendor always does the right thing at the right time without a company representative to exercise oversight of the contract and motivate the contractor and its employees.

It is the responsibility of the customer to direct and focus the outsourced association. The contract monitor retains control of the relationship with the security service vendor, assures success of the outsourced service by making it a business arrangement, evaluates the contract in business terms, and enforces accountability through clearly defined service levels.

9

Outsourcing Security Investigations

Investigations conducted by private parties have their roots in more than 100 years of U.S. history. Private investigation is a burgeoning business. It would be rare to search the yellow pages in any telephone book in this country and not find a private investigative firm. These agencies provide a multitude of investigative services to a broad spectrum of industries, businesses, and other entities worldwide. Many have become specialized in the services they perform, such as forensics, executive protection, and electronic surveillance countermeasures. Others supply more traditional and generalized services. This chapter discusses a few suggestions regarding strategies a potential client might consider in outsourcing investigative tasks to third-party contractors.

WHY OUTSOURCE SECURITY INVESTIGATIONS?

At some point, companies inevitably need professional investigative services for a multitude of purposes that range from a simple preemployment inquiry or worker's compensation case to large investigations, such as when a poison was intentionally introduced into bottles of over-the-counter pain reliever being sold to the public. Other investigations have international implications and concern an endless list of serious offenses against various companies, necessitating use of highly sophisticated investigative skills and technology. The number of specialized investigative requirements that arise in the normal course of business in a typical company demonstrates the need for a professional resource that is immediately available to a broad range of clients.

Many executives believe that any manager using common sense and judgment can follow a logical course of inquiry to resolve an issue. Whereas this opinion may have some credibility in solving most business problems, it has little worth when addressing an actual investigation of matters that may have civil or criminal implications. These require special expertise and knowledge of the various laws and procedures applicable to investigative techniques, including search and seizure, interview and interrogations, laws of evidence, false imprisonment, conduct of surveillance, and other procedural issues and statutory requirements. It is not unusual for managers to begin an investigation into a reported offense and later find that the matter is beyond their level of investigative competence. They either request police assistance or employ a private investigative agency to resolve the problem. By this time, the manager may have tainted evidence otherwise admissible in a prosecution or taken other improper actions that would alert the culprit to the investigation and allow him or her to use countermeasures to thwart investigators and avoid detection.

INTERNAL INVESTIGATIONS

In a general sense, a corporate investigation usually is initiated on receipt of information or an occurrence that indicates a wrongful act has been committed that would adversely affect the assets, personnel, or image of a company. A manager, usually the company's security manager, reviews the information or evidence and decides whether further investigation is warranted. A company has a legal right to conduct its own investigations into matters of interest that might affect it or, if conditions dictate, to summon the appropriate law enforcement authorities if it determines a crime has taken place within their jurisdiction and is of a nature that warrants their action.

CONSIDERATIONS RELATING TO PROSECUTION

When initial inquiries have substantiated that purposeful wrongdoing has occurred, company executives decide whether to seek prosecution if the offense is of a prosecutable nature and if the identity of the allegedly guilty party is determined. If a company decides to pursue prosecution, it is prudent immediately to involve the company's legal counsel and the law enforcement agency that conducts the investigation. The reason is that if management conducts its own investigation and collects its own evidence, the manner in which the investigation is performed and the methods of collecting and preserving evidence are subject to scrutiny and challenge by defense attorneys.

If evidence is tainted in a corporate investigation, or if the investigation was not conducted in precise compliance with prevailing laws and procedures, the prosecution can easily fail. Constitutional guarantees apply only to the force of government, and management prerogatives of a private entity are not always bound by these guarantees. These facts, however, are not always accepted by juries as excuses for actions of management the jury may see as prejudicial to a defendant. If the investigation is conducted entirely by a public law enforcement agency with the directed assistance of management, the outcome of the investigation is likely to be more favorable.

INITIAL CONSIDERATIONS FOR SELECTING AN INVESTIGATIVE FIRM

There are different situations in which a company might want to conduct an internal investigation and refrain from soliciting external assistance. One example might be a case of such proprietary sensitivity that management does not want to relinquish control of the investigation or its results to an outside source. The sensitive nature of the investigation demands that it be conducted in a professional, objective, and accurate manner. Few businesses have a professional investigative staff who can be dedicated to a time-consuming investigation. When no professional in-house resources are available to a business organization, the alternative is to outsource the investigation to a security service that has such competencies. As with selection of any type of security service, the investigative resource should be selected with a responsible degree of care. The question again arises whether it is more advisable to solicit the services of a national agency or a local, independent private detective service.

Some experts assert that a local agency dealing strictly in investigative activity has local contacts, informants, and other sources of reliable information available to them that can be used to the client's advantage. Because the independent investigative service does not engage in any other service and does not have to retain many full-time employees, its overhead expenses are expected to be lower than those of a full-service security organization. Consequently the cost of engaging such a service is less than that of hiring a full-service security organization, which has high management expenses. This opinion has some merit, but a client should exercise diligence when selecting an independent investigative firm to determine the level of competency, experience, and skill of the investigators to be assigned to the client and the professional manner in which the investigation is to be managed.

The anticipated scope of the investigation is an important consideration. A determination should be made regarding whether the local agency has the staff and capabilities to expand the scope of the investigation if it becomes necessary. For example, if the matter under investigation involves a complex fraud case, the services of a certified professional accountant, or at least a competent fraud investigator, may be required. Determining the scope of any investigation is difficult, because unexpected events might suddenly emerge and affect the course and outcome of the proceedings.

QUICK ACTION AND RESPONSE

A company usually does not have the time or opportunity to formally solicit bids for the occasional incident investigations and to prepare a statement of work for this sole purpose. Time is essential when performing an investigation because information and evidence can be distorted or obliterated. When it is determined that an investigation in a particular matter should be initiated and outsourced to a competent supplier, the concerned company must act quickly to choose a qualified security firm and start the investigative action with minimum delay. If the company has negotiated a guard service contract with a full-service security firm, provision of investigative services may have been included in the security statement of work. When such a service has been previously negotiated, the security service provider naturally is included with any investigative assignment as part of the contract. If the contractor does not have the expertise to conduct a particular investigation, language should be included in the original statement of work that permits the client to contract another investigative firm. In this event, the company that needs investigative services must discuss its requirements with other potential service providers on an individual basis and make its selection accordingly.

INVESTIGATION IN DIFFERENT VENUES

The use of a local licensed security firm to conduct investigations within the concerned facility or in the immediate locale of the client may be advantageous when a professional service can be provided. If the investigation requires action in a distant office of a large company, the corporate office may retain control of the investigation and select a national firm to perform the investigation in each of the locations involved. In this case, each facet of the investigation is controlled and coordinated through a central office and precludes communicating with different agencies in a number of locations. The same concept applies to multinational companies.

A case study involved a U.S. firm with facilities throughout the world. A major fraud case was discovered in the company's office in the Malagasy Republic, and the alleged perpetrator had fled the country. The individual was traced by a national investigative firm through several countries and ultimately found three months later working at a French bank.

INTERNATIONAL INVESTIGATIONS

International investigative firms are useful in providing supplementary assistance to U.S. corporate security directors who are responsible for safeguarding corporate officers traveling abroad. The foreign offices of international security firms can provide security staffs, arrange accommodations in safe hotels, provide bodyguard and armored limousine service, expedite passage through airports, provide translators, supply valuable local intelligence and information to the client, and perform other services in a country that might be beyond the immediate capabilities of the U.S. corporate security personnel.

CONSIDERATIONS FOR SELECTING
AN INVESTIGATIVE FIRM

The need to investigate a major incident may force a company to act so quickly that it may not have the time for formal selection of a private investigative agency. Regardless of the urgency of a situation, the company must prescribe certain qualifications and skills necessary for an agency to perform a professional investigation in such cases and to outline a preliminary scope of investigation. These precautionary questions might include the following:

1. Is the investigative firm licensed in the state where the investigation will occur?
2. Are the investigators being assigned to the client licensed where state law requires?
3. How long has the agency been in business?
4. Are the assigned investigators full-time employees of the agency? If so, how long have they been employed?
5. What are the investigators' professional qualifications, experience, and skill to perform a specific investigation?
6. Will the assigned investigators remain on the case until its completion?
7. Does the investigative firm have adequate liability and casualty insurance in the amounts prescribed by the client?
8. Is the contractor willing to execute an indemnity and insurance agreement with the client?
9. What quality assurance controls will the contractor's management exercise over continued professional performance of the investigation?
10. At what frequency will the client receive agents' reports, status reports, management reports, or other miscellaneous reports specified by the client?
11. What rates will the potential contractor charge the client? Basic rates, overtime rates, travel expenses, mileage and other incidental expenses? All expenses should be itemized with reasonable receipts required as specified by the client.

After receiving answers to the questions, the client should do the following:

1. Carefully examine the credentials and experience of prospective contractors who claim specialization in undercover investigations and conduct inquiries with business reporting agencies with regard to a potential contractor.
2. Hold in-depth discussions with the selected contractor in which objectives are clearly articulated and comprehensive plans are made with regard to the best method of inserting the investigator into the workplace, the conduct of the investigation, and alternative emergency plans.

3. Insist on reviewing the credentials, experience, and qualifications of the investigative personnel being assigned to the contract. Investigators with no experience in undercover investigations should be rejected regardless of any other attributes that qualify them to fit in with the organization.

4. Reserve the right to make the final determination regarding the suitability of the investigator to fit into the work environment.

5. Be prepared to expand or reduce investigative activity as conditions warrant.

6. Allocate sufficient funds to the operation on the basis of projected costs.

7. Make discreet internal arrangements to effectively insert the investigator into the workforce.

8. Appoint a single point of contact to interact with the contractor's controller.

9. Determine the identity of persons within the company, without regard to position, who must have knowledge of the operation. It is imperative that these be kept to a minimum consistent with operational requirements.

10. Execute a binding contract with the contractor that defines the objective of the operation, prohibited actions, frequency of reports and communications, emergency procedures, anticipated milestones and schedules, breakdown of costs, and that the vendor and its agents are independent contractors. Ensure that the contractor provides documentary evidence of all required insurance and indemnification.

11. Be prepared to involve law enforcement as conditions warrant.

12. Carefully evaluate agents' reports and determine the progress of the investigation to decide whether the investigation should be continued or terminated.

CONFIRMING CONTRACTORS' CREDENTIALS

Investigative contractors are reluctant to disclose the names of clients for reference purposes unless previously agreed by the former client; in some states, this privilege is protected by law. Therefore it is unlikely that a potential client will be able to confirm past performance of the contractor. When this question becomes an important issue, the client can request a Dunn and Bradstreet report and check civil court records and Better Business Bureau files with regard to adverse information or litigation involving the potential contractor. A word of caution is necessary with regard to the use of Dunn and Bradstreet reports. Information contained in these reports is provided largely by the contractor and may not always be regarded as reliable and accurate. Such reports should be corroborated.

BACKGROUND INVESTIGATIONS

There are many instances in which a company may want to investigate the background of applicants for employment. A company also might want to verify the qualifications of a current employee being assigned to a position of extreme trust and sensitivity from a position of lesser responsibility. A current employee also may be the subject of a separate company investigation, and certain lifestyle or background facts are pertinent to determining culpability or involvement.

The company has two main options. It can conduct an investigation through in-house resources or contract with an outside investigative firm. Companies that have no structured investigation staff and frequently need to perform background inquiries often subscribe to computerized data and investigative companies that provide software at relatively low cost that enables the customer to conduct personnel and business background investigations, skip tracing, credit reports, and provide other information sources on a national basis to an approved customer by means of personal computer. Although this system allows individual companies to conduct low-cost investigations and inquiries with in-house staff, background investigations continue to be a substantial market for private investigative firms. One reason may be a client's desire to have the investigator make personal contact with former employers of an applicant and with neighbors and associates, review public records, and develop leads that result in a comprehensive investigation.

CONTRACTING BACKGROUND INVESTIGATIONS

Contracting with an investigative firm to perform background investigations provides the client with greater opportunity to go through a more structured process to select a professional service. There usually is no urgency to negotiate a contract with a service contractor in these cases, and the client can adhere to the complete selection criteria of preparing an investigative statement of work, soliciting and evaluating bids and proposals, and awarding a contract to the selected vendor.

Companies that engage in such contracts usually enter into an agreement in which the contractor performs a predetermined number of investigations within the contract period or performs personnel investigations as an as-needed service on a retainer basis. Some private agencies are reluctant to accept a contract to perform a certain number of investigations a year. If, for example, a client negotiates a contract in which the contractor is obliged to perform 100 investigations a year and the client inundates the agency with 90 investigations in 1 month but has no further investigative needs for the next 8 months, the contractor may experience a severe and disruptive staffing problem.

Some agencies may subcontract investigations to part-time investigators. This practice presents a quality-control problem, because the contractor can rarely guarantee the competencies of the third-tier investigators. A company with only an infrequent or sporadic requirement for investigative services might select a preferred vendor and request any investigations through a purchase order agreement. These arrangements do not require a specific contractual relationship and do not commit the client to a specific number of investigations or use of a specific contractor for a particular time period.

RELEASE OF INFORMATION

Regardless of the type of investigative service they deem best for their purposes, clients are advised to ensure a proper release form is executed by applicants for employment to authorize the possessor of information to release the information and records to the investigator. In many cases, such release-of-information statements are a part of a company's employment application form, as is notification that the applicant may be subject to an investigation to confirm qualifications, education, and other statements made by the applicant. This type of release-of-information statement may be suitable for some purposes. It is more acceptable, however, to have the applicant sign a separate release-of-information statement. The investigator presents this document to the individuals releasing the information, who may want to retain a copy for their files.

Companies that use the services of a private investigative agency should be aware of legal considerations that affect them. One of the most important laws, since the Homestead Law, enacted to control the activities of these agencies is the federal Fair Credit Reporting Act. This is a far-reaching act that encompasses a broad range of organizations, particularly those that provide to a requester information relating to a person's credit, background, character, reputation, lifestyle, and other traits and habits. It places a burden on the requester to notify the subject of the investigation that such an inquiry is being performed by a third-party agency and to advise the subject of the type of information being sought, if the subject so requests.

If an applicant is denied employment, promotion, insurance, or credit, or experiences other adversarial action as a result of an investigation, the applicant must be informed that rejection was based on information contained in the report and must be told the identity and address of the reporting agency that provided the information. Many restrictions imposed by the Fair Credit Reporting Act do not apply to companies that use an in-house investigative staff, unless stipulated by state or local law. Ethical licensed private investigative agencies are intimately familiar with the laws and controls that affect their business and make an assiduous effort to comply with them. A company considering use of a third-party investigative agency should consult with legal counsel to ascertain laws that apply to investigations and the precise actions the company should take to comply with those laws.

UNDERCOVER INVESTIGATIONS

One of the most controversial types of investigations performed by business is the undercover investigation. These are often used when a company has reason to believe that unlawful or unauthorized acts are occurring on its premises but facts and evidence cannot be obtained through conventional investigative activity and it is expected that an undercover investigation may provide substantial results. The controversial nature of these investigations may be based in part on the legacy from early days in which "spying" on employees was a normal course of business (see Chapter 1).

Other reasons are the secrecy with which the investigation must be performed and the adverse consequences of any compromise of the investigation or disclosure that it is being conducted. Such knowledge may build resentment and lower morale among the employees with whom the agent worked, incur lawsuits regarding invasion of privacy, and expose agents to physical harm if their identities become known to the persons involved in the wrongdoing. Concern for the safety of agents is heightened if the investigation is focused on use or distribution of drugs in the workplace or similar activities that may be associated with gangs, organized crime, or other groups prone to violence.

Labor unions traditionally have condemned undercover investigations as potential surveillance of employees and interference in the activities of the workforce. If agents are expected to work in a bargaining unit, extraordinary measures must be taken to ensure that they do not engage in or report on activities normally construed as unfair labor practices and prohibited under laws that protect collective-bargaining activities. These issues should be outlined in detail to investigators, and appropriate training should be conducted to ensure agents are clearly familiar with what constitutes prohibited practices.

When a company decides that an undercover investigation is appropriate, usual practice is to engage a contract service. This is preferred to employing an independent individual as an undercover agent on a contract basis because of the extensive planning, coordination, and control that have to be performed by the company rather than a professional contractor. As with other security services being contracted, it is imperative that the client select a professional contractor with specialized experience in providing qualified personnel to conduct an undercover investigation.

Selecting an Undercover Service

The requirement for a qualified investigator cannot be understated. In too many instances, a contractor may promise that its most professional investigator is completing an assignment and will be available to undertake a new task within several days. In reality, the alleged professional investigator may not even exist, and the delay in beginning an assignment is to allow the provider to advertise and hire personnel who may have no investigative experience. It is incumbent on the client to demand that the contractor provide documented evidence that ensures the individual being assigned to the investigation possesses the appropriate training, experience, and other qualifications necessary to perform the task effectively.

Putting the Right Person in Place

In addition to possessing the qualifications, undercover investigators must have the capability to blend with the educational, economic, and cultural environment in which they are to work. It is inappropriate to place a clearly nonmuscular person with uncalloused hands on the docks to work as a stevedore. Agents must be accepted by coworkers, gain their confidence, and be able to establish a casual and social association. Agents must have the knowledge, experience, and credentials for the position in which they are to be placed in the client's organization and effectively assume the role they are expected to play.

Planning the Undercover Investigation

Substantial effort and coordination must occur between the client and the service provider to plan and implement an undercover investigation. The first consideration is that no person regardless of position be made knowledgeable of the investigation unless there is absolute need to know regarding the operation. This often is a difficult situation to resolve because almost every supervisor and executive can claim a need to know that an undercover operation is in progress. The company manager or executive in charge of the investigation should exercise exclusive authority to determine who is entrusted with such information. Need to know should be interpreted as a determination that disclosure of the information to a prospective recipient is required to allow the recipient to make an essential operational contribution to the investigation to ensure its confidentiality and effectiveness.

Placing the Undercover Agent into the Workforce

A second consideration is the manner in which the undercover agent is to be introduced into the workforce. The normal procedure is to insert the undercover agent into the employee population in accordance with regular new-hire employment procedures. This necessitates that the client find an appropriate opening in a position that allows the investigator access to the target areas but with enough flexibility to move about as necessary without causing suspicion. If no such opening is available, the client may have to exercise credible ingenuity to create one. The investigator applies for the position and provides suitable credentials to prove his or her qualifications for the position. In some cases, the client may find it appropriate to use discreet influence on personnel managers to encourage employment of the agent.

The Agent's Cover Story

It is essential that the client work closely with the security service contractor to develop a plausible cover story for the agent. The cover should be closely associated with the agent's actual work experience, education, lifestyle, and other personal facts that can be generally substantiated. The question arises regarding anonymity of agents and whether it is appropriate that they use their own identities when applying for a position in the company. Many corporations require birth certificates, social security identification, and other documents for proof of U.S. citizenship and personal identity. This fact makes it generally necessary for the undercover agent to use his or her actual identity unless other measures are sanctioned and taken by the client, in concert with the contractor, to establish a false identity for the agent. This places an additional burden on undercover investigators to ensure that they do not drive a personal vehicle registered to them, carry their own identification, or engage in any activity that might betray their real identities while performing their investigative functions.

Controlling the Undercover Investigation

An undercover investigator has a single point of contact to report findings, receive instructions, and control the investigation. This is usually not an employee designated by the client but a representative of the contractor's organization. That the company has relinquished control of the investigation to the contractor may be a disadvantage to the client in one sense and an advantage in another. The individual controlling the investigation must be available to the agent on a 24-hour basis and be intimately aware of the circumstances in which the agent is working to be able to give proper direction and advice. Most contacts between the controller and the agent are accomplished by telephone to an unlisted number and monitored by the controller. Meetings often are held at discreet locations away from the workplace. Written reports are sent to a post office box to avoid any connection between agent, controller, and client. It is inappropriate for a company employee with no experience with an undercover operation to be in the position to act as the controller. The client's surrender of control of the investigation to the contractor often is frustrating, because it frequently appears that nothing substantial is occurring in the investigation and that the client has little power to accelerate the operation.

Undercover operations frequently are prolonged and require much time and patience. Because clients equate much time with much money, they become much impatient if nothing positive appears to be happening after weeks or months of investigative operation. Contractors who do not adhere to a rigid code of ethics attempt to ameliorate this condition by suggesting that the agent is very close to solving the matter and urging that the investigation continue for another two or three weeks to gather the information and evidence the client requires for successful conclusion of the investigation. After the time lapses, the contractor may offer an excuse as to why completion of the investigation was delayed but that it is now positively on the track of the culprit and certainly can complete the investigation within another short time. Depending on the limits of the contractor's propensity for developing excuses, the investigation can be drawn out far past the time when it should have been terminated.

The decision to end an undercover investigation can present a dilemma to a client if there have been no substantial results within a specified period of time. However, when an investigation is terminated before valuable evidence is found, the entire cost of the investigation is wasted. This decision can be made much easier when the investigation is performed by a qualified investigator and professionally controlled by the contractor in close coordination with the client.

In many cases, the contractor does not explain to the agent precisely what the mission is or identify any suspects. Consequently the agent may wander aimlessly into the assignment, reporting every inconsequential observation and musing at length on issues that have no relevance to the investigation or concern to the client. This is confusing to the client, particularly if great effort had been made to place an experienced investigator to make association with the suspects in a timely manner. It is confusing to investigators, who may have no idea what nature of evidence or wrongful activities they are looking for or whom their targets might be. Contractors may state that they prefer their investigators not be advised of a specific objective so that they may remain impartial and observant of all activities, or some other similar reason. In many situations, it is an excuse to allow inexperienced investigators to become used to their surroundings and then be gradually directed to the real objective. A contractor may try to extend the length of the investigation for additional profit. The client may find in reading the agent's reports that the contractor has actually placed an experienced undercover agent in the workplace or has merely recruited a neophyte who is being directed by the controller.

Involvement of Law Enforcement

Client and contractor have to plan for the possibility of involvement of law enforcement authorities at some point in the investigation. When the evidence of wrongdoing is of such a nature and extent that the appropriate police organization should be advised at the onset of the investigation, the client may confer with law enforcement to determine whether it may be more appropriate to place an undercover police agent in the workplace. In other cases, the police may approach business management and ask to be allowed to place an undercover investigator on the premises on the basis of information disclosed in other police investigations. When such requests are made and the company acquiesces, control of the investigation is entirely within the purview of the law enforcement agency, and the company has little control of the outcome. This can include serving of warrants on company property and arrest of employees at the workplace. Situations such as this are rare if the company is assured of the safety of other employees and agrees to the action.

Companies should be aware that they cannot legally prevent a law enforcement agency from serving warrants within their premises if the agency is determined to do so. Because the objective of a police organization is detection of crime and apprehension and prosecution of criminals, the police have little interest in matters relating to the protection of assets of the corporation. In view of these considerations, management may give careful thought to involvement of police in an undercover investigation unless it is entirely warranted and justified by prevailing conditions or the company's insistence on prosecution. If involvement of law enforcement authorities is deemed appropriate, it should be discussed with the selected contractor as soon as the issue arises.

Cost Considerations

The cost of an undercover investigation is often exorbitant depending on the length of the investigation and the number of agents assigned to the case. The company must understand that it has to pay investigators the normal salary or hourly wage consistent with the position they hold in the assignment plus a management fee to the contractor. The client must pay payroll taxes and any other supplemental costs if the hourly or daily wages are not sufficient to meet the agreed on rate paid to the investigator. If the undercover investigator must be brought from another city, the client must bear the costs of transportation, meals, and lodging. It is not unusual for an undercover investigation to continue for an extended period. Depending on the prevailing rates, the number of agents assigned to an investigation, and the contractor's fees, the aggregate expenditure may be many thousands of dollars. Although some investigations have been extremely successful, others have yielded results that were much less than desired.

A company contemplating an undercover investigation should weigh the benefits and potential adverse consequences associated with such activities. The company might do the following:

1. Evaluate other methods of gathering factual information and evidence regarding suspected events or activities involving the corporation or its employees.
2. Consider the probability of achieving successful results with an undercover investigation operated by a contractor and the liabilities and hazards associated with the nature of the investigation.

Although the foregoing recommendations are not all inclusive and cannot guarantee a successful conclusion to an investigation, they may assist business executives in such an undertaking and help them make informed decisions regarding implementation and performance of an investigation.

SUMMARY

This chapter discusses reasons why an outsourced undercover investigation may be an appropriate course if information or evidence of a wrongdoing or other unauthorized actions cannot reasonably be determined by means of other investigative processes. It outlines the many considerations an organization must weigh before making such a decision, including evaluating cost against anticipated results. Also discussed is the manner in which undercover investigations often are performed. This helps potential clients understand the process and emphasizes the absolute need for selecting the most professional investigator on the basis of quality and expertise rather than cost.

10

Outsourcing Security Services Overseas

The surge of U.S. businesses into the international community and the globalization of the economy have caused an explosion in travel and residence in other countries by U.S. citizens. Many of these persons have little or no overseas experience and have only minimal awareness of the risks to which they might be exposed. Proactive companies with facilities and employees in foreign countries are addressing their concerns by taking prudent measures to provide their employees with a safe working environment and to protect their assets. In many respects, this involves outsourcing of security services to in-country resources. The purpose of this chapter is to provide some of the considerations associated with this activity.

The topics in this chapter are addressed in a general sense, because there are myriad differences between countries and in their political, economic, cultural, and social environments. It would be impractical to attempt specific differentiation. Although much of the material in this chapter has been provided by various sources, some of the information is derived from the author's personal experiences.

PREDEPLOYMENT EDUCATION

Business travelers routinely go to countries that are new to them. All too frequently they have little or no familiarity with the different ways of life they experience. Unseasoned travelers often expect little change from their lifestyles in the United States. They expect the privileges and rights to which they are accustomed in the United States to prevail the new environment. All too often, they are wrong. The problem is that they have entered cultures that may be entirely different from their own and they have not been educated in the differences or how to cope with them. Progressive companies realize this fact and have instituted educational programs to enlighten employees traveling outside the United States. The programs create an awareness and help acquaint the employees and their families with the way of life in the new country and provide them with the information they need to protect themselves from the risks they might face. These companies have found value in placing an informed professional in place rather than letting employees flounder on their own. The consequences of having an uninformed employee in a new country might be disastrous to the employee or cause serious embarrassment to the company. Because few businesses, especially smaller companies, have an in-house staff to compile educational material, they resort to third-party providers for this service.

The demand for such educational and private intelligence information regarding conditions in foreign countries has resulted in the emergence of a variety of companies with the expertise and resources to deliver competent services to meet this need. Among these are private intelligence companies with worldwide resources and some national full-service security contractors and others that provide current information regarding the state of affairs in foreign countries and make situational risk assessments in those countries. The advantage of outsourcing this function is that subscribing clients can access such information through a personal computer link with the contractor and obtain country profiles, executive updates, and newsletters on any country covered by the provider. Other sources also supply information to aid a company in developing these educational programs. These include Brigham Young University and the U.S. Department of State, which provide information either at no cost or on a paid subscription basis.

SECURITY PLANNING IN AN OVERSEAS ENVIRONMENT

In-country security contractors have an important role in helping U.S. businesses develop security plans for the safety and security of their facilities and employees. Whether these in-country services are locally owned and operated companies or foreign branch offices of a U.S. national security firm, they have resources available and valuable to U.S. businesses operating overseas. This includes intimate knowledge of specific conditions within the country the average business executive might not normally possess or even consider when attempting to develop security plans for the overseas organization.

It is vital that a company employing the services of an in-country security firm, where such firms are authorized, select a professional contractor with whom it can form a close alliance and on whom it can place a great deal of trust and dependency. A security contractor is going to be one of the most important resources a company has in developing and implementing the security plans for the overseas organization. Suggestions regarding selection of an in-country contractor are addressed later; it is mentioned here only to amplify its importance.

In the discussion of use of in-country security contractors, it is assumed that a U.S. company is developing security plans for a new overseas facility in which no proprietary security management or other defense resources are present. In this case, the company goes through the same basic processes applicable to designing a security program in the United States. However, there are vast differences, because the threats and vulnerabilities change greatly depending on internal influences in the country where the facility is located. An in-country security contractor can be invaluable in identifying issues and offering competent services and guidance to mitigate adverse effects.

Among the many issues a U.S. company must consider in developing an overseas security plan are changing environments of the particular countries, because the threats come from different sources in each country. These threats may accelerate or decline depending on the religious, governmental, and social infrastructures within the various areas. With the exception of a few countries, U.S. businesses face a heightened security threat, particularly in developing countries and areas experiencing cultural or religious conflict or economic and political instability. By contracting with an in-country security service provider to make a comprehensive situational assessment of security threats that include the preceding considerations, clients are supplied with information that gives them a better perspective on external influences they may confront within the country.

Such an analysis includes a profile of any existing groups within a country that might pose a threat to the company. It also should provide insight regarding the probability that the company and its employees will be identified as a target of such a group. If the probability is high, the company might consider increasing the funds allocated to the security effort and encourage more involvement with the security contractor. The reason is that although hostile activities within a country may be dormant at the time, the situation can change instantly. This necessitates that the company maintain a state of readiness and awareness and have the capability to respond to the situation, including the establishment of an in-depth evacuation plan if it becomes necessary to remove employees from an endangered area. In many cases, the security contractor can assist the company in designing emergency plans that include arrangements for evacuation transportation, personnel recovery, hostage negotiation, and other contingencies that might accompany hostile actions that threaten the safety and security of the company and its employees.

A company may place great dependence on the security services contractor. However, regardless of the closeness of the alliance between client and contractor, the contractor has commitments to other client organizations to which it must also provide support and service. In the event of an emergency, the contractor's resources might be stretched very thin, and the contractor may not be able to provide extraordinary services to every client. In expectation of this event, the client should have devised its security plans in such a manner as to be as self-sufficient as possible with the understanding that the contractor provides the standard mutually agreed contingency services.

SELECTING THE APPROPRIATE CONTRACTOR

When a company chooses to outsource its security services overseas, the client naturally considers many of the same basic issues it would in contracting in the United States. The exception is that the overseas service might be expected to provide a different range of activities. The alliance between a client and a contractor outside the country is a valuable investment if the right contractor is selected.

Whether the client chooses a local, in-country independent contractor or contracts with a U.S. security firm with international branch offices depends on the resources available in the country and the company's determination of which service is best for it. U.S. businesses operating in other countries and with headquarters or home offices in the United States might find it beneficial to negotiate a contract to protect the foreign facilities with a United States–based international security firm.

The management policies of an international security firm govern the quality of performance provided by the overseas offices. In this respect, a higher level of service and control is anticipated. This provides the U.S. client with an avenue of recourse to resolve problems with its U.S. contractor rather than having to deal with a foreign contractor on a day-to-day basis. It may allow the U.S. client to hold an international security service provider to a standard of contractual performance for services being provided abroad equal to the standard for services performed in the United States. By contracting with a U.S.-based international security service, the client may find it can facilitate enforcement of the provisions of a contract in a much easier manner than struggling through the legal vagaries of another country to demand compliance with a contract with a foreign provider.

U.S. businesses with facilities and employees in various countries might find additional benefit in contracting with international security organizations that have multiple offices in the same countries. With offices in the same countries as the client, the security service contractor might better serve the client because there will be uniform policies and procedures, making it easier for the contractor to enforce the stipulations of an existing contract in each location. With a presence in various countries, the security service contractor probably has established communication links between offices and can share information valuable to the client. An additional advantage to contracting with an international security firm is that the home office of the U.S. firm can coordinate the security activity and resolve problems at foreign facilities by merely communicating with the security contractor in the United States without having to consider time zones or experiencing communication difficulties that are common in many countries.

Although many multinational companies have found definite advantages in dealing with international security firms, others have found disadvantages. The main disadvantage is that nothing is ever as it seems. As with national security firms operating in the United States, the level of service and efficiency of operation of each office depends on the competency of the management in those offices and the varying levels of resources available to them. These differ from one location to another. Although uniformity with contract performance might be expected from an international security firm, it might not always be produced. Another consideration that affects the uniformity of contractual performance is that laws, cultures, religions, and political and social conditions differ between countries and might substantially influence the quality and manner in which security services are to be performed. For example, the quality of an outsourced security officer force in Great Britain may be much different from that of one in Somalia.

The option of a client outsourcing security services is to investigate the competencies of local full-service foreign security companies. Such independent organizations provide many of the same services as international security companies, such as VIP protection, background investigations of employees and domestic workers, escorts, security assessments, and security officer forces, provided these tasks are stipulated in a statement of work. A local firm may have closer connections in the community than an international firm and be more acquainted with the specific political and cultural influences and the attitudes of the populace within their sphere of operations. These issues are quite beneficial to a company in maintaining a state of readiness for their security programs. Another consideration is that a local firm may be able to provide the same services as an international service provider at less cost because its operating expenses and managerial fees are not expected to be the same as those of an international contractor.

For U.S. companies with a centralized security organization in the United States that administers the security programs of its facilities in foreign countries, it might be difficult to deal with a variety of independent security providers in different locations. There are different contracts and different managerial philosophies with each company. Communication between the security department at the U.S.-based headquarters and the security contractors in various countries is difficult to achieve. A possible solution for such a situation is for the centralized security organization to relinquish control or administration of the contractor's operation to the highest executive at each of the company's overseas facilities.

In some countries, such as Turkey, security officer protection must come from one of two sources—local police or private security officers hired as full-time company employees. Private security officer contractors, either local or foreign based, are not authorized. In such locations, the U.S. firm may seek advice regarding security concerns from the U.S. Department of State or a regional security officer at the U.S. consulate in the country concerned.

PROCUREMENT OF SECURITY PRODUCTS

When it is necessary for U.S. managers to procure security products in a foreign country, it is natural that they write product and system specifications in accordance with those with which they are familiar. It is not unusual to expect that these be patterned on U.S. components, products, and standards. Although U.S. products are in abundance in the overseas market, in some countries these might not always be readily available or may not be compatible with other products in the foreign markets.

Several years ago, a British firm conducted an exhaustive marketing study in Europe with the purpose of introducing a highly technical and sophisticated access-control and intrusion-detection system developed and produced by a U.S. company under ownership of the British company. The interesting result of the study was that the European marketplace had no substantial interest in the U.S. product. It was more concerned with promoting its own countries' products and rejected any competition by the U.S. system, regardless of the advanced technology of the United States. This study is mentioned only to illustrate one of the reasons why some types of U.S. technology may not always be immediately accessible in some countries.

If a U.S. company purchases in-country products, it might exercise caution with regard to the procurement of security systems. The business may not receive the same level of product service and quality it expects from vendors in the United States. Once a business has determined a need for a security system or product in a foreign country, the process of determining the quality of the product is related to the size of the security expenditure being considered. The greater the expenditure and complexity of the system or products being purchased, the more study and evaluation should be given to selection of a vendor. The following questions should be considered:

1. If it is a product rather than a service, does the vendor provide a warranty? If so, what is covered and for how long?
2. Does the vendor provide the names of clients previously served and a description of the services provided?
3. Does the vendor provide firm costs and convincing evidence of competence to service what the vendor sells?
4. If a system or product is being provided, does the vendor supply information about the product failure rate?
5. Does the vendor have the capability to maintain the product or system or offer technical upgrades as the technology of the product changes? Under what terms and conditions are these services to be performed?
6. If the system being purchased is a security system used to protect a sensitive area, does the vendor have the capability to provide rapid response to correct any deficiencies or failures in the system?
7. Does the vendor have replacement components or parts in stock for immediate replacement?

Although these questions may sound simplistic and are of the nature that most procurement managers would take for granted in the United States, it can be a far different situation in other countries. Work practices, obligations to customers, availability of material, technical competency, ability to meet deadlines, and many other considerations must be resolved when planning for the procurement and installation of security products and systems for overseas facilities. These change from one country to another and can cause frustration when well-planned activities quickly go awry because a small factor the planners took for granted was not addressed.

SUMMARY

This chapter looks at some of the considerations a U.S. firm may confront when preparing security plans for protecting a facility and employees in a foreign country. Although some of the basic considerations regarding security planning are universal, threat levels, threat sources, vulnerabilities, and other factors that exist in foreign countries are a source of concern to those responsible for developing the plans. The planners have to have much more information than normally expected for plans developed for facilities in the United States.

This chapter recommends a U.S. firm form an alliance with a full-service security contractor in the country in question. This contractor should have knowledge and expertise that might not otherwise be available to the client. To choose a U.S. security firm with international affiliations or select an independent, in-country full-service security provider is a determination that the client has to make in deciding which type of service is most applicable to its unique requirements.

Procurement of security systems and products from an in-country vendor is discussed briefly, because these considerations may be different from those in the United States. The purpose of this chapter is to illustrate that differences between the United States and other countries have a profound effect on the way U.S. businesses protect themselves in the foreign environment.

11

Outsourcing Security Consulting Services

The years in which companies retained large in-house security organizations, including high-level management staffs and specialists, appear to be on the decline. As companies peel away their support services, many of their leading and more obvious security functions and capabilities are being outsourced to contractors. Because administration of an effective security program involves a broad range of disciplines and processes, a number of the in-house skills and knowledge that once were available to the company may no longer be there for them. It is possible that third-party sources that have contracts for specific tasks, such as security officer forces, investigations, VIP protection, and other functions may not be expected to have the expertise or qualifications to provide the objective professional advice a company needs from time to time to resolve specific matters. One option in resolving this dilemma is employment of an outside security consultant to fill the void.

This chapter reviews the methods and considerations a client may use in selection and engagement of a security consultant and the technical, managerial, and operational contributions the consultant might provide to an organization.

THINKING ABOUT USING A SECURITY CONSULTANT

There are times when a company is confronted with unique security problems or concerns within its wide scope of responsibilities, and it may need special advice to resolve them. There are two options for obtaining assistance—resort to in-house staff to provide a solution or employ an outside security consultant.

Resolving complex issues might be beyond the capabilities of the in-house staff, and they may not be able to provide an objective and definitive solution to the problem. For example, if a comprehensive study must be performed with regard to expenditure of capital funds for installation of a highly technical security system, the in-house staff may not possess the technical qualifications necessary for objective appraisal of the project. An independent consultant with specialized, thorough, and current knowledge of the technology involved is of particular value in such a case because he or she can provide an unbiased and technically sufficient evaluation on which to base an informed decision.

A company might resist employment of a consultant. In some cases, the individual responsible for security administration may view employment of a security consultant as a reflection on his or her competency. In other instances, executives may not have the degree of confidence in the services of an outside consultant they have in their own employees. A third cause may be that because executives do not have the control over a consultant they exercise over their own employees, they fear a consultant's report may reflect adversely on their managerial processes. Competent executives should not allow these concerns to influence the decision to employ a security consultant. It is the consultant's function to resolve problems and provide advice and assistance to a company to improve its security posture and have a positive influence on the internal relations of the client.

WHY USE A SECURITY CONSULTANT?

As U.S. business continues up the slopes of organizational change to meet the growing needs of its customers, so the needs change for professional guidance and counseling. Professional security consultation has become an integral discipline within the security industry. It is gathering momentum as businesses turn to outside experts to provide services not available internally. There are myriad individual reasons for an organization to retain the services of a security consultant. The basic reasons are as follows:

- To obtain expert advice
- To control costs
- To obtain an objective point of view

The first reason relates to assisting a company executive to make informed decisions based on the professional expertise of the consultant. The second reason is associated with the first. Often it is necessary for an organization to undertake security-related projects that are labor intensive and may be beyond the capabilities and competencies of the internal security organization. To achieve the desired results, it is more cost effective to employ a professional consultant for a temporary period than to assign an internal staff member who may lack the qualifications. The staff member may spend much time and effort only to obtain unsatisfactory results or not complete the task at all. It might be much more productive to employ an outside expert to complete the project promptly and professionally and at less cost than for an internal employee. The third reason—to obtain an objective point of view—is highly important. A subjective or biased evaluation of a situation or condition has little value to an executive attempting to make a major decision regarding the expenditure of funds to safeguard valuable assets or to provide a secure work environment for employees.

CHOOSING THE RIGHT CONSULTANT

As with selecting any outsourced contractor, the client must be assured that a consultant must be the right fit for the work to be undertaken. Consultants should possess the same broad qualifications as many other executives being considered for employment. They must have experience, education, professional credentials, and the ability to establish interpersonal relationships with others and exhibit integrity. Consultants must be able to understand and adjust quickly to the culture and management philosophies of the organization they serve.

The client should examine other attributes a consultant should possess, such as whether the consultant understands completely the scope of work to be performed. Consultants who do not have this understanding waste their time and the client's money exploring issues irrelevant to the project and negate the purpose of the assignment. The consultant selected should have an established reputation and success with other clients. The client might question whether the work performed with past clients was similar to the tasks required by the company and whether the former client would retain the consultant again.

There are four general categories of consultant. First are individual experts who operate independently and have no affiliation with any vendor or service provider. Second are small consultant businesses with a variety of specialists, and third are large organizations that offer a broad range of consulting services. The last category is considered the most proliferative in the United States. They are security vendors or private investigators who advertise themselves as security consultants. For example, in Texas, one of the few states that regulates the security consulting profession, there are approximately 380 licensed security consultants, and all but four of them are salespeople. Unquestionably, many of these organizations have qualified experts in some fields. Because these experts are representatives of vendors or service providers, they might not be able to provide an objective approach to an assignment, or they may be pursuing a second agenda of marketing their products or services.

Some individual independent consultants may engage in a wide range of managerial and operational consultations, whereas others focus on more specialized areas, such as retail security, hospitals and retirement communities, educational institutions, and other specializations. An individual consultant cannot be expected to have complete expertise in all disciplines. This also applies to small consultant firms, which might employ specialists but require additional assistance to deal with requirements of an assignment beyond those available within their own staff. In these cases, the independent or smaller consultants may often use other experts to complete a complex assignment.

Unless they are generally oriented to providing security consultations, larger management consulting firms do not always have the capabilities and expertise effectively to undertake security consulting assignments. This situation is changing as some of these organizations recognize the demand for such services and are adding security experts to their staffs. A client anticipating employment of a larger consulting firm should require that the qualifications and credentials of the individuals who actually perform the assignment be provided for the client's review and investigation.

DESCRIBING THE STATEMENT OF WORK

In many cases, a security consultant is retained when conditions or problems exist within an organization and there are insufficient internal resources available to resolve them. A company also may evaluate its security posture proactively to ensure that its assets are being protected and that a secure work environment is being provided. The scenarios in which a security consultant might have a role encompass a wide range of activities and disciplines too extensive to mention here. Regardless of the assignment, the objectives and tasks of a security consultant must be defined in sufficient detail for the consultant to determine the extent of work to be performed, where it is to be performed, the time limit for completion of the assignment, specific issues to be addressed, and an array of other information necessary for the consultant to bid and perform the work. These topics are described in a statement of work issued to prospective consultants before submission of a proposal.

The consultant must understand the work to be accomplished. It is equally important that the client understand what is to be done and articulate it in the statement of work. For a consultant, undertaking an assignment for a client who has not completely identified its objectives and requirements may prove unsatisfactory for both client and consultant.

In some instances, a statement of work limits the consultant to a specific issue. For example, the client may want only an evaluation of the security of a single building within a complex or might confine the consultant to examination of parking lot security. The client should remember that other insidious influences or conditions might exist within the organization that indirectly affect the subject under review. By limiting an assignment to a very specific target, clients may be denying themselves information about more serious problems a consultant might have uncovered had he or she not been so restricted. If the consultant discovers such situations and brings these to management's attention, the client should be willing to broaden the scope of the assignment to include other areas of review as conditions warrant.

EVALUATING PROSPECTIVE CONSULTANTS

Before submitting a statement of work, some clients may interview prospective consultants to review the assignment and allow the consultant to raise questions regarding the scope of work. If the assignment concerns a study of facilities, campuses, or other locations, the consultant might take the opportunity for on-site review of the area for familiarization purposes. Although a client may have been provided with the curricula vitae of perspective consultants during initial communications, a personal interview allows face-to-face discussion of the consultant's qualifications and experience.

Although many consultants have a natural propensity for the work, very few are born into the profession. They acquire expertise through years of education and work in a career at progressive levels in which they develop a wide range of experience in solving problems and supervising people. For example, it may be difficult for some consultants to relate to a security officer or office clerk unless he or she has had experience dealing with functional levels of employees and understanding the perceptions associated with the work. Consultants should have supervisory experience in which they gain knowledge in managing performance and resolving complex and diverse problems by making decisions and accepting accountability for them.

It is preferred that a consultant have some years of experience as an executive on the policy-making level and have experience in business administration, advanced management techniques, and dealings with contemporaries and customers. It is extremely difficult for a consultant to work with a client executive or appreciate the executive's concerns unless the consultant has had similar experiences. A client can make these determinations by interviewing the consultant to satisfy concerns regarding the candidate's capability to perform the work required.

After receiving a statement of work, the consultant provides a cogent proposal, usually written, that defines his or her understanding of the scope of work to be performed and describes the following:

- What will be done
- The methods the consultant will use to accomplish the task
- Where the work will be performed
- A beginning and ending date for performing the work
- Names and qualifications of associates of the consultant who might assist in the work
- The fee for the work

In evaluating the proposal, the client may gain insight into the professionalism of the consultant. The proposal might reflect the consultant's organizational abilities, communication skills, approach to solving problems, and other qualities in which the client may have interest. The evaluation process should include all the other factors a client considers when selecting a contractor (see Chapter 6).

THE CONTRACT

Many companies have developed consulting contracts that have passed legal sufficiency in the states where they apply. These contracts generally cover issues such as the following:

Service to be rendered by the consultant
Rate of payment for services
Reimbursement for expenses
Invoicing
Confidential information
Independent contractor stipulations
Use of work products
Designation of client and contractor representatives
Liability
Applicable laws
Scope of agreement
Additional work
Assignment agreement
Termination of contract

In other cases, the client may accept a contract prepared by the consultant provided that all conditions and stipulations are mutually agreed and provided that the contract has legal sufficiency.

The client has the expectation that the consultant executes a nondisclosure agreement in which both parties agree to protect and keep confidential material deemed to be proprietary or sensitive to each party's interests and is identified in the agreement. Because a consultant may have worked for a competitor of the client, the consultant may be requested to sign a conflict of interest statement in which the consultant acknowledges that there are no facts that would give rise to any organizational conflict associated with the work for the client.

THE ASSIGNMENT

The client should provide access to its staff, records, and resources, because such access may relate to or facilitate the consultant's operation and fulfillment of the obligations. If the consultant is being required to study a facility or its operations, the client should arrange for the consultant to have access to the premises at all hours. It is frequently necessary for a consultant to view a facility or inspect its security operations during normally closed hours and during hours of normal operations. If there are areas in which the consultant's presence is prohibited, such as a classified area at a defense contractor or governmental facility, these restrictions should be explained to the consultant before the beginning of the assignment. The problem sometimes can be mitigated by assignment of an escort to a consultant who needs access to these areas.

The client should provide the consultant with adequate background information on the company, management philosophies, the organizational structure, and certain other basic information the consultant might need. Consultants should be introduced to key personnel with whom they might have some association during the assignment.

The client should designate a point of contact with whom the consultant has direct connection and provide the necessary liaison between the company and the consultant. The functions of the appointed individual are to assist the consultant in collecting data and providing other assistance as needed. Some companies designate a point of contact who is also in a position to authorize changes in the scope of work in the contract and expenditure of additional funds to accommodate the changes.

In many cases, the client has no objection to having its workforce or customers aware that a security consultant has been employed and is to be working on the premises. Some clients advise managers and employees of the fact and through internal communication introduce the consultant and explain his or her general purpose. This aids the consultant because the client's personnel may feel more inclined to be straightforward and cooperative if they are interviewed by the consultant. For other clients such an open approach may not be appropriate, and the client keeps the consultant's activities known only to a select group. This requires special consideration and communication between client and consultant to determine the method of operation the consultant might use to achieve the desired results.

As the assignment progresses, the client should expect the consultant to make periodic status reports regarding the progress made. These reports should be made to all persons who have an interest in the work being done. In most cases, these status reports are made orally to advise the client of the work being done at that time. The reports also cover whether the work is on schedule and on budget, define any problems encountered, and identify issues that indicate additional work should be undertaken or that changes should be made in the scope of work.

The frequency of status reports depends largely on the size and complexities of the work being performed. If the work is being done in short phases that may require 7 to 10 days to complete, a status report can be given at the completion of each phase. If the assignment is more complex, the client and consultant should agree on the frequency of the reports required. Periodic status reports assist management in ensuring that the consultant's work remains focused on the scope of work. They also provide the opportunity for management to find conditions that have to be corrected before the assignment is completed and eliminate any surprises. If a consultant observes any condition requiring immediate or emergency attention, these should be reported on discovery.

THE FINAL REPORT

The final report is usually specified as the deliverable the consultant is expected to produce. At minimum, this report defines the results achieved and identifies any additional work that should be done. If the assignment included a survey of an organization's security posture, the report should reflect the consultant's findings and recommendations for improving existing security deficiencies and conditions. The report should include any findings that indicate that additional work should be done. For example, a consultant retained to conduct a facility security survey for a large corporation, discovered that the company's emergency disaster and business recovery plans had been neither tested nor changed in more than 20 years. In fact, many managers were unaware that such a plan even existed. During that period, the company's operations had changed substantially, making the original plans virtually obsolete. Realizing that the absence of current emergency plans could be disastrous to the company, the consultant was awarded a follow-on contract to assist the company in developing and implementing new plans.

Sometimes a client may not want a written report but wants only an oral report of the consultant's findings. This may be a cost-savings measure in eliminating the expense of a documented report, or it might be because of the sensitive and confidential nature of the assignment. In such cases, the client should define this requirement in the early stages of negotiation with the consultant.

The client should expect to conduct a final briefing with the consultant at the conclusion of the assignment. This briefing is usually conducted by the consultant with members of top management and includes discussion of all salient features of the written report. Although a final report should be clear and self-explanatory, questions in the minds of some executives may need further clarification, explanation, or justification. A final briefing provides the opportunity to have these issues definitively resolved.

CONSULTANT COSTS

Professional consultants fees are usually competitively balanced. Some, however, range from being above those acceptably charged within the security industry to those that are quite low. A low bid generally occurs because an individual who claims to be a consultant has other sources of income, such as those derived from being a sales representative of a security service. These bids should be viewed with caution because the consultation effort often is used as a marketing device. In this case, the work done by the consultant can be slanted toward procurement of services or products the client does not actually need.

There are other reasons why a consultant may bid low. Some may operate in a particularly concentrated market in which competition may be quite heavy, and it is necessary that they submit low bids to maintain their competitive edge. Others may bid low to maintain a number of clients who keep the consultant busy during periods of relative inactivity. Although these are ethical reasons, a potential client should be cautious of consultants who bid low and work slow. This is often purposeful, because the assignment can be protracted to increase the billing. In some cases the client can avoid this by stipulating a date by which the assignment should be concluded.

As with other professional disciplines, there are no bargains in the consulting field. There is a distinct relation between consultants' fees for services and the quality of the services. A number of factors influence consultants' fees, such as location and duration of assignment, environmental hazards, personal hardship, and travel and living expenses. The costs charged by individual consultants and by large firms must compensate for overhead expenses, such as office, clerical assistance, proposal expenses, nonreimbursed travel costs, taxes, advertising, and other administrative costs associated with the business. The basis for higher billing rates by some larger consulting firms is the higher salaries and benefits paid to employees and management and the increased overhead costs. Engagement of consultants at times may be a considerable expense to the client depending on whether an independent consultant or a large, multidisciplined organization is used.

Regardless of the type of arrangement made for payment of services, consulting work is usually broken down to an hourly basis. This fee is based on the actual time required to complete the assignment. If a project is to extend for months and involve complex issues, the client and consultant may not be able to arrive at an accurate completion date. In this case, the consultant may charge a fee for actual hours worked with no final fixed amount defined. In addition to this agreement, there are three other general types of payment arrangements, flat fee, not-to-exceed fee, and retainer fee.

A *flat fee* is usually negotiated in advance of the work to be performed and is based on an agreement between consultant and client regarding the number of hours estimated to complete the assignment. In many cases, the consultant may agree to a flat fee only when the work to be done is relatively straightforward and can be controlled by the consultant. Flat-fee arrangements are usually avoided if the assignment is complex and might require others in the client company to participate in the work or if other conditions exist that are beyond the consultant's control. In such a case, the consultant has to absorb cost overruns. Conversely, if the consultant completes the task at a cost less than the agreed-on rate, he or she collects the entire fee.

Experienced consultants can estimate the length of time and level of effort required to complete an assignment on the basis of their understanding of the scope of work and their experience with other clients with similar requirements. In this case, the consultant presents a proposal with a *not-to-exceed fee*. Clients find this type of arrangement suitable, because they know at the outset their financial commitment to the consultant. If the final costs are lower than anticipated, the client is billed at the lower cost. If the costs are higher than the estimated amount, the consultant absorbs the extra costs as a result of an erroneous estimate. When a consultant offers to accept a not-to-exceed fee and the client changes the scope of work and increases costs, the fee for extra work should be negotiated with the consultant.

A *retainer fee* is usually paid when a client uses a consultant on a regular basis. In this arrangement, the consultant agrees to be available to the client for a specified number of hours or days each month. Because there is usually an ongoing relationship with the client, the fee might be at a discounted rate because the consultant may or may not work the time specified. If the consultant is not called on to work the specified hours, the fee is still collected because the consultant had committed that time to the client. Retainer fees are often for a specified time, such as one year, after which the arrangement is renewed or terminated.

SUMMARY

This chapter reviews the use of consultants for occasions when a company requires expert advice from an objective source that is not readily available inside the organization. Use of a consultant offers executives a degree of professionalism in approaching problems at less cost than having to add employees to their staffs. This chapter reviews methods with which a company can select the proper consultant for the specific requirements and offers suggestions regarding achievement of a successful relationship with the consultant.

12

Has Outsourcing Gone Too Far?

This book discusses a number of issues regarding outsourcing security services. The remaining question is how far into the future will outsourcing reach? The trend to outsource continues to increase steadily as companies divest themselves of functions they consider to be extraneous to their core business. Whether outsourcing places a company in a stronger and more competitive position has yet to be determined. It may take years to establish the alliances and partnerships with contractors that outsourcing companies hope to accomplish.

IS OUTSOURCING A UNIVERSAL CURE?

Outsourcing of services, if it is inconsistent with the core competencies of an organization, may not be the panacea many contemporary managers and executives believe it to be. There are many good reasons for a company to retain support services by employees because it works best for them. For example, a defense contractor producing satellites may use its own printing department to comply with a collateral contractual requirement to develop and print technical manuals or blueprints classified in the interest of national security and require personnel security clearances for persons who have access to them. In many areas, a company might find it difficult to locate a printing firm with the capability to protect classified material or with employees who have the clearances necessary for access to such material. It is imprudent to outsource this task to a contractor. The same problem applies to companies with security officer forces that perform sensitive duties in areas where there are limited outside resources.

ESCAPING OLD PARADIGMS

For decades, many U.S. businesses were self-sustaining entities in which all operations and support services were integral parts of the organization controlled

entirely by internal management. Every facet of service, whether it was an employee cafeteria, maintenance department, janitorial service, or security guard
force, was often provided by internal organizations and employees. Cost was not
always an issue because these expenses could usually be controlled internally, as
could the quality of service. The accountability for cost and quality of the services
and their supervision was internal to the organization and was considered to be
a valuable benefit to the company because any requirements received immediate
attention without third-party involvement. Many of these organizations were influenced by a paternalistic style of management that encouraged the use of employees to provide the necessary services to the company.

Executives were comfortable with that situation and considered it a worthwhile cause because they believed it provided the level of control necessary to
operate an efficient organization and fostered a loyal and productive workforce.
Employees enjoyed the security and benefits that this condition offered in the
belief it would continue and they would be able to retire in relative comfort from
a long period of steady employment. Unfortunately, time and events proved both
executives and employees wrong.

NEW ENVIRONMENTS

In recent times, domestic and international events such as global competition,
new economic treaties and trends, and countless other changes and influences
have created an environment in which U.S. corporations feel the need to revolt
against the old styles of doing business and to reinvent themselves to remain
competitive in the new global market. They have had to restructure the organizations and reengineer the processes to produce greater quantities in better, faster,
cheaper ways while improving quality and elevating their customers to a supreme
level of ecstasy with their services and products.

In rethinking their methods of operation, companies have seen that the old
paternalistic management philosophies have to be scrapped in favor of operations
that are lean and mean. Among other issues, this means an expensive labor base
must be minimized while essential services are maintained to support the activities of the business and protect its assets. Following a natural sequence of events,
companies have found they can replace many functions previously performed by
employees and outsource the displaced activity to specialized vendors.

Outsourcing has become a solution for many companies in the throes of
downsizing. Some executives have resorted to the Yellow Pages philosophy,
which is that if a needed service can be found in the telephone directory, it can
be outsourced. Proponents of using external resources claim countless business
advantages to the practice. For example, by using a contract security officer force,
clients can save approximately 30% of the cost of a proprietary service and provide economic gain to the user. A properly selected vendor effectively monitored
by a client can provide services equal in quality to those of an in-house guard

force and supply a broad spectrum of technical resources and capabilities that might otherwise be beyond the reach of a proprietary security officer force.

Outsourced services have been perceived as a mechanism to free clients' management to concentrate on issues essential to the core business rather than spending valuable time supervising an activity that might have only a collateral association with the main business objectives of the company. These perceived advantages have spurred the initiatives of countless companies to outsource to contract vendors many services and functions once performed internally.

THE GOVERNMENT STORY

One of the most notable organizations that has had remarkable success in forming alliances with contractors, including those providing highly differentiated security and law enforcement duties, is the U.S. government. Many government agencies are privatizing the investigations of the backgrounds of persons nominated for personnel security clearances and admission to military academies. Notable among these agencies is the National Aeronautics and Space Administration. For years, NASA has fostered alliances with its contractors and has privatized many security and law enforcement responsibilities to security service providers. Part of the agency's success has come about because the agency is committed to extremely high levels of quality performance and excellence and demands the same pledge from their contractors. In certain instances, these alliances have become so strong that many contractor employees working at NASA facilities and installations frequently associate themselves more closely with the customer agency than with their own employers. Associations such as these work only when there is a consistently strong bilateral effort to ensure success and there is harmonious communication between the two parties.

It is essential that clients closely monitor contractors' activities to ensure that there is no degradation of service and that they impose pecuniary sanctions if the expected quality of service is not sustained.

SIGNS OF OUTSOURCING REVERSAL

The question arises whether outsourcing has gone too far. Although The Outsourcing Institute has projected that outsourcing will continue well into the future, other signs reflect a gradual reversal of the outsourcing trend through a reduction in the quantity and types of services contracted to external markets. This is manifested by a growing number of executives expressing disenchantment with the quality of security contractors who profess more than they possess.

The level of training given to contract security officer forces may not reach the standards required of an in-house operation, or the level of attrition within a contract service may be disruptive to the client's business, particularly if the contractor was selected on the basis of a lowest bid. The close alliances between the client and the vendor that may have been expected in the beginning of an outsourced service often fail to reach fruition because of the exaggerated expectations of a client or a lack of credible data to justify beginning such a union.

Outsourcing has been affected by the number of mergers and acquisitions within many U.S. businesses, in which a large variety of companies with different core disciplines and technologies are brought together as a consolidated organization. This may result in a condition known as *vertical integration,* in which a manufacturer is able to supply its own components and services from its newly acquired in-house resources rather than outside contractors. If this course continues, it is possible that the outsourcing trend may continue to decline in certain disciplines. A few Fortune 500 companies have reverted to use of proprietary security officer services. It is arguable, however, whether this is a true indicator of a course of action that increases over time. To make such a determination, it is necessary to examine closely each company that has abandoned a contracted security service to define the reasons for the re-transition to a proprietary force. In many cases, the contracted service may have been an inappropriate fit for the requirements of the company, the contractor's performance was not monitored effectively, or the wrong contractor was chosen for the wrong reasons.

In many cases, businesses that discarded a proprietary security officer force and made the transition to a contract service succumbed to the allure of less expensive security service and the perceived benefits of a reduced workforce. As companies began to realize substantial cost savings by converting to security guard providers, making the transition became a trend that spread through U.S. industries. These industries were searching desperately, and in some suicidally, for any means to reduce overhead and remain competitive.

The imperative to save expenses has made it necessary for some businesses to reexamine their security requirements and adjust them to meet financial constraints. Unfortunately, many such decisions have been made by managers concerned primarily with cost reduction rather than maintaining practical security measures needed to protect the assets of the company. As a result, many compromises have been made in security programs. It is not surprising to find that the expense of maintaining and supporting a proprietary security officer force exceeds the advantages it may have provided.

An attempt to ameliorate security concerns has been made through the demand for quality-assurance commitments on the part of contractors and expectations for close alliances on the part of clients. Companies that closely monitor the security contract and work diligently to make the alliance work have appreciated success with vendors. The lack of similar success in other organizations may be the result of a lack of bilateral dedication to creating a successful alliance between client and contractor. Establishing such alliances may take several years and require strong effort by both contractors and clients, and their employees. In these evolutionary times, business concepts, philosophies, and management are changing almost daily. Acquisitions and mergers are constant, including contractor firms, and employees are striving to keep their heads above water while they cope with "initiative overload," the condition in which initiatives are put forth faster than they can be implemented. These are a few conditions that make it difficult for many companies to stay the course in attempting to embrace alliances with contractors. Although this philosophy may be paramount today, it might be put aside for other emerging initiatives tomorrow.

Some companies have outsourced services to the point where it has become difficult to control and administer the number of contracts they have issued. Monitoring and administering contracts is a time-consuming process. It requires procurement actions, accounting procedures, auditing, quality assurance, billing processing, regulatory and contractual compliance, legal issues, and other tasks that require intensive action to maintain and support a large contractor base. A collateral issue is that as contractors' costs increase, the financial benefit to the client declines. Because a large number of companies outsource because of cost effectiveness, there may come a point at which the cost of outsourcing exceeds that of maintaining in-house support services.

QUALITY AND EXCELLENCE

Another issue that affects the growth or decline of outsourcing security services is the ability and willingness of contractors to commit themselves to the true premise of quality and excellence. Many security contractors have achieved this objective, especially a number of the larger enterprises. In general, however, the experience of security contractors has been with buyer-seller types of contracts. It has been only in recent years that such a large-scale effort has been made to change those relationships and make the transition to associations that emphasize quality and excellence and are of longer duration. The length of a contract in which a partnership is being attempted is an important factor. It takes at least one or two years for the benefits of the new association to become evident.

If a national contract is negotiated, the results of an alliance may vary from one location to another. Each jurisdiction is administered by different field office managers whose perceptions of the meaning of quality may be different from those of the client. To minimize these problems, there must be a clear understanding regarding the requirement for consistent application of quality-assurance efforts supported by the contractor's national headquarters.

Local managers of contractor field offices must be educated in the methods of establishing and perpetuating solid long-term relationships with their customers. This requires that many of them be retrained in new management techniques and rethink the manner in which they market their services and perform them. Re-education should include a level of training that parallels the new business management strategies being taught to potential clients to enable clients and contractors to communicate on the same level and to form a better understanding of the forces that drive them. The horizon of thought of contractors' local managers should be broadened to allow them to think more in terms of long-lasting business relationships with their customers than on one- or two-year contracts to sustain their businesses. These managers must have a deep business orientation and experience and broad security knowledge. It is no longer sufficient to employ persons with extensive law enforcement or similar security-related work experience and expect them to relate satisfactorily with persons who have years of business management experience and are well versed in new management concepts.

Business groups assert that because this is an age when Americans are becoming more entrepreneurial, it only makes sense to use the services of contractors. Although outsourcing is being accepted more by business, it is facing some opposition from organized labor, which is struggling to increase its ebbing numbers. Regardless of what may appear to be indications of growing reluctance to outsource certain functions and services, and considering that some businesses have reinstituted proprietary security forces, there probably will be no appreciable decline in the number of security services being performed by contractors within the next decade. This assertion is based on the supposition that as more clients learn the art of preparing the groundwork for an outsourced service, develop the ability to select the most appropriate and qualified vendor, and learn to effectively monitor the service, the benefits of using security contractors will become increasingly clear.

SUMMARY

This chapter discusses some of the reasons that make outsourcing a preferred strategy for an increasing number of clients. It also addresses a few of the causes that have encouraged a number of companies to slow down in their rush to outsource everything not directly associated with their core business. Although these causes and conditions will always be present, few question that provided a contractor is selected carefully and responsibilities and tasks are specifically defined, outsourcing security services will continue to offer a viable and cost-effective option for the business community, as it has for more than 150 years.

Appendix

Samples

1. Statement of Work

2. Format for Proposal

3. Invitation to Bid Letter

4. Nondisclosure Agreement

5. Bidder Qualifications Questionnaire for Security Officer Services

6. Background Investigation Authorization

7. Professional Consulting Services Agreement

8. Conflict of Interest Statement

Note: All samples are provided for the convenience of the reader and are intended only as specimens, to which there are many alternative styles and examples. These samples should not be construed as having legal sufficiency in all jurisdictions. An attorney should be consulted by readers who choose to use these specimens either in whole or in part.

SAMPLE 1: STATEMENT OF WORK

1.0 General Provisions

This statement of work defines the specifications that describe the services to be provided by a competent commercial security service company; hereafter referred to as the contractor. The services specified herein are to be provided to [Client] _____ at facilities located within the State of _____; and hereafter referred to as the client. The contractor shall be responsible for providing qualified security officers, in the number and for the hours specified, to perform services as detailed in these specifications. The security services shall be pursuant to the client's contract in writing between the parties.

1.1 Licensing

The contractor shall be duly licensed in the state in which services are performed to provide the services of a commercial security officer service and the services of the investigation agency as may be required. Implicit in this licensing requirement shall be the capability to successfully qualify selected personnel for the carrying of concealed weapons should the client subsequently require their service and the state or territory grant this privilege.

Should the contractor fail to comply with any state, county, city, or territory licensing and performance requirements and should the contractor receive written notification of noncompliance for the State, or County Governments, the client shall be advised of such notification within twenty-four hours of the contractor's receipt of notice. The client shall then have the right to immediately terminate the agreement.

1.2 Independent Contractor

The contractor and its agents shall offer services to the client as an independent contractor and shall accept the requirements of these specifications as the requirements of an independent contractor necessary to perform the function of a commercial guard service at a professional and sustained level of adequate service.

1.3 Insurance Requirements

The contractor shall present evidence of insurance on the types and amounts required by the state, city, county, or territory and in terms and amounts satisfactory to client. Included in the required insurance coverage shall be the following:

- *Worker's Compensation* in accordance with applicable federal and state laws.
- *Employers Liability and Occupational Disease Liability* in the amount of $_____ per occurrence

- *Comprehensive General Liability* including but not limited to contractor's protection insurance if subcontractors are used. Completed operations liability in the amounts of $_____ each occurrence for bodily injury; and $_____ for property damage.
- *Comprehensive Automobile Liability Insurance* including, but not limited to, coverage for nonowned vehicles in the amount of at least $_____ for bodily injury and $_____ for property damage.
- *Fidelity Insurance* in the amount of $_____ per incident for the actions of the contractor and/or its agents.
- *False Arrest Insurance* for false arrest, false imprisonment, libel, slander, invasion of privacy in the amount of $_____ per incident.
- In all insurance coverages in the liability and casualty area, the contractor shall provide documented evidence naming the client as the name insured, prior to acceptance of the contract. The contractor shall execute a "hold harmless" agreement as appended.

1.4 Contractors' Investigation of Project

Contractors shall visit each site at which security coverage is to be provided and take such other steps as may be reasonably necessary to ascertain the nature and location of the work and character of the site, location and scope of post performance requirements, and other general and local conditions that may reasonably be projected to exist, at the commencement of service. Failure to do so shall not relieve bidders from responsibility for accurately estimating the degree of difficulty and cost of successfully performing the assigned tasks. The client assumes no responsibility for any representation, concerning the nature of work or the working conditions made by its officers, agents, or employees, unless committed in writing in the Contracts Documents by an appropriately authorized person.

1.5 Discrepancies and Interpretations

Should a contractor find any discrepancies in, or omission from any of these specifications or is in doubt as to their meaning, they shall advise the client, who will issue necessary clarifications to all prospective contractors by means of addenda or revisions as may be deemed appropriate.

No interpretation of the meaning of the specifications will be made to any contractor orally and be considered binding on either party. Failure of a contractor to receive addenda or interpretation will not relieve the contractor from any obligation.

1.6 Client Reservation

The client reserves the right to reject any or all bids, to waive minor informalities in any bid, or to make an award in the best interests of the client.

2.0 Administrative Requirements

The requirements set forth in this section pertain to the form and substance in which the work shall be administered. In this regard it shall be the responsibility of the contractor to adhere to these administrative requirements and to provide the client with timely notification of noncompliance. For purposes of this specification, timely notice shall be interpreted as within five business days with the exception of subsection 1.1.

2.1 Cost Disclosures

The contractor shall include in the bid all cost data relating to the performance of all services specified herein. Included in this cost data may be, at the client's discretion, the following cost factors:

> Direct labor cost by individual or post
> General and administrative expense, including but not limited to:
> > Uniform cost
> > Equipment costs
> > Maintenance costs of uniforms and equipment
> > Tax burden
> > Supplies expense

Additional cost data may be required depending on services performed. For purposes of this specification, if the cost data is assembled in the normal course of business and does not represent an undue and/or unreasonable expense, that data shall be made available as requested in accordance with the schedule defined above.

2.2 Markup Control

The contractor shall be restricted to a markup over direct labor costs of not more than _____%. This shall be inclusive of all General and Administrative Expense, Tax Burden and profit, licenses, permits, uniforms, noncontributory fringe unemployment compensation, initial training cost, retraining, and insurance. The contractor shall have the right to present for client's consideration temporary increases or decreases in the markup percentage within a _____% to _____% range based on specific training requirements identified but not included herein.

2.3 Turnover Control

The contractor shall exercise reasonable and responsible diligence in providing the client with security officers who are qualified to perform the services required. In this regard, the contractor shall make all reasonable efforts to minimize attrition among trained qualified security officers to the extent that turnover in the security force shall not exceed _____% per annum or _____% in one quarter. Should turnover exceed these limitations the contractor shall, at their own expense, provide all training previously provided as necessary to make the replacing security officer possess a level of skill equal to the security officer who has terminated service. Notwithstanding the above provision, if the client requires the removal of a security officer for reasons other than the ability to competently perform required services; non- or malfeasance in the performance of duties or matters relating to fidelity of an individual security officer, the contractor shall bear the training expense beyond that required for basic qualifications and on-the-job training. Exceptions to these provisions may be made, in writing, by the client based on individual circumstances.

2.4 Overtime Authorization

In relation to wage and hour law requirements that shall be adhered to, the following overtime provisions shall apply to services performed under this contract:

- Overtime rates equal to one and one-half times the contract security officer rate shall be paid for service in excess of forty hours per week. Should a security officer perform overtime services requiring skills other than for which they are currently compensated, the overtime billing rate shall apply.
- Overtime rates equal to one and one-half times the contract security officer rate shall be paid by the contractor for a negotiated number of holidays.
- Overtime resulting from the contractor's inability to provide personnel in quantity and quality acceptable to the client shall be paid by the contractor at one and one-half times the contract security officer rate.

2.5 Nonperformance Penalties

The contractor shall agree to accept a financial penalty to 1% of the contract cost incurred by the client for nonperformance of substantial contract provisions. The penalty percentage is subject to increases in 1% increments up to a maximum of 5% for repeated uncollected performance failures. The 1% penalty shall apply only to chargeable hours in which the substantial nonperformance existed and only to the posts and level of service affected by the substantial nonperformance.

Substantial nonperformance shall include, but is not limited to, the following areas:

- Failure to comply with wage and hour regulations
- Failure to maintain percentage maximum on turnover control except for those instances in which the client and contractor mutually agree that the turnover is justified
- Failure to comply with pre-employment qualifications and investigations regarding applicants

- Failure to report an incident
- Failure to comply with federal, state, and county regulatory requirements
- Failure to perform services for any reason

Each instance of substantial nonperformance shall require documentation sufficient to prove to a reasonable and prudent person that the nonperformance occurred. Each instance shall be individually reviewed by the client and the contractor, and the penalty shall be exercised only when both mutually agree as to the substance and cost of the nonperformance and the degraded level of client service that occurred. In instances in which mutual agreement between the client and contractor do not exist, an arbitrator shall be selected and an arbitration conducted pursuant to the codes of the American Arbitration Association, and the costs incurred for the services rendered will be borne by the party whose position was not upheld.

2.6 Replacement of Equipment Provisions

The client shall, from time to time, make equipment available for the use of the security officers in the performance of the contracted services. The contractor shall bear the cost of repair and/or replacement of such equipment rendered inoperative because of the misuse and/or abuse of the contract employee using the equipment or due to a failure to provide the contract employee with training sufficient to operate the equipment in a normal, safe, and effective manner. This provision shall not apply to equipment failure mutually agreed by the client and the contractor as having occurred as a result of normal use or wear.

2.7 Documentation of Incidents

The contractor shall be responsible for providing both a written and an oral report of any incident that occurs on any shift by the close of that shift period. This report shall be provided to the shift supervisor. An incident is defined as, but not limited to, the following:

- Any apparent or suspected criminal attack exercised against the client, its assets, or personnel, including the employees of the contractor assigned to the site or any authorized visitors thereon.
- Any criminal or civil charges brought against the contractor or its personnel as it may relate to the contracted service
- Any apparent trespass of the client's property
- Any verbal or physical confrontation resulting between a contract employee and a client employee or guests or visitors of the client
- Any performance failure of the contractor
- Any federal, state, or county regulatory requirement in which the contractor is in noncompliance

- Any equipment or system failure associated with the performance of the contracted service
- Any fire or unsafe condition existing within the client's environment and observed by or reported to a contract employee, and the emergency actions taken by the contract employee to eliminate or ameliorate such conditions
- Any incident in which procedures governing the safe and orderly operation of the site are violated

2.8 General Reporting Requirements

The contractor shall provide to the client information in documented form as identified in substance and frequency set forth below. These reporting requirements shall not be considered exclusive, and the client may, at its discretion, identify other recoverable documented information relating to the contracted service.

Substance	*Frequency*
Billing	Bimonthly
Names of personnel assigned to the contract	Weekly
Percentage of personnel turnover	Quarterly
Hours of service performed by post and compensation rate	Monthly
Summary of service performed by post and compensation rate	Monthly
Training (classroom or on the job) completed by hours, substance of training, and personnel	Monthly
Cost analysis of service	On request
License renewal and certificate of insurance conforming with government regulations	Annually

3.0 Personnel Matters

The requirements set forth in this section pertain to the quality and performance capability of security officers assigned to this contract service. In the event specific requirements set forth herein are in conflict with any government regulations, the government regulations shall govern.

3.1 Candidate Qualifications

The contractor shall consider the following qualifications as indicative of entry level skills necessary to assimilate the training requirements and perform services at an adequate and sustained level. Notwithstanding these entry level requirements, experience will be considered as a potential equal or better entry level requirement based on individual review of a candidate's qualifications. The following qualifications shall be considered acceptable for presentation to the client:

- Minimum age of 18 years
- High school diploma or equivalent written examination
- Successful completion of a written, validated examination indicative of the candidate's ability to understand and perform the duties to be assigned.

    Note: Examinations must meet criteria that fairly measure the knowledge or skills required for the particular job or class of jobs the candidate seeks or that fairly affords the employer a chance to measure the applicant's ability to perform the job or particular class of job.
- No record of convictions for criminal offenses
- A valid motor vehicle operator's license when operation of motor vehicle is required
- Physical capability to do the job assigned
- A personal background of employment and personal experience indicative of the candidate's capability and inclination to represent the employers and client's credibility, and integrity in the performance of a life/safety service to the client's employees, visitors, and guests
- Ability to pass a pre-employment and drug/alcohol screening test

The contractor shall conduct a background investigation of each candidate to be presented to the client for consideration. The investigation shall include, but not be limited, to five years of employment and neighborhood experience of the candidate. The background investigation will be an adjunct to any "paper and pencil" integrity tests given to the candidate as a matter of the contractor's hiring and personnel screening policies.

The client shall accept a contractor manager's certified report that a background investigation was conducted in accordance with the stipulations stated herein and that an impartial adjudication revealed that no derogatory information was disclosed during the investigation that would be inimical to the client's interests by assigning the candidate to the contract. This report shall be made orally to the client at least 24 hours prior to assignment, followed by a written certification within the first thirty days of employment.

3.2 Presenting Candidate Qualifications

The contractor shall present a copy of the candidate's qualifications for assignment to the client's service. The contractor shall certify that the materials submitted are the results of the contractor's investigation, testing, and examination and represent true and factual information.

3.3 Client's Report of Approval

The client reserves the right to review the candidate's qualifications for assignment to the client's service. If the client fails to advise the contractor that the candidate is unacceptable for assignment to the contract within twenty-four business hours of presentation of the candidate's credentials, the contractor will assume that the candidate is acceptable. Exceptions to this stipulation are identified in Section 3.11.

3.4 Minimum Training Before Assignment

The contractor is responsible to provide the training set forth below to each candidate before assignment to the client's service, or provide evidence acceptable to the client that the candidate by background and experience has an equivalent skill level to that established in the training program. This training is provided at the contractor's expense.

Instructors will be provided by the contractor. Training materials will be jointly supplied by both the contractor and client. The preassignment training will include the following areas, but not to the exclusion of other areas. The term *preassignment* shall be interpreted as that training given to a contractor's employee prior to assignment to the client's facility.

- *Module 1: The Security Responsibility (2 hours)*
  The life/safety responsibility
  Maintaining effective enforcement
  Maintaining proper appearance
  Bearing and appearance
  Report writing and documentation requirements appropriate to client's
    needs

- *Module 2: The Protected Environment (1.5 hours)*
  Description of client's environment
  Details relating to the functioning of the life safety and security systems
    on site
  Description of the client/employee relationship that must be maintained
  History of client's security experience relating to past incidents at
    multiple locations

- *Module 3: Legal Powers and Limitations (3 hours)*
  Philosophy of prevention versus apprehension
  The concept of timely intervention in a developing situation
  The limitations of arrest powers and the client's requirements in these
    matters
  The use of force and the need to establish ability, opportunity, and
    jeopardy to self and others
  The limitations on search and seizure and the client's requirements in
    these matters

- *Module 4: Standard Operating Procedures (3 hours)*
  Description of entry-level job responsibilities pertaining to assignment to
    client's premises
  Basic administrative practices of the client

Familiarization with client procedures and documentation practices
Identification of the client's access-control and alarm systems
Handling confrontations on client's premises

- *Module 5: Emergency Practices (2 hours)*
  Identification of types of emergency situations that may predictably occur
  Description of emergency systems including the following:
  (1) fire detection, (2) fire suppression and evacuation, (3)
  familiarization with emergency procedure, (4) fire, (5) bomb threat,
  (6) power failure, (7) vehicle accidents, (8) injury/illness, (9)
  workplace violence

- *Module 6: Review (1 hour)*

3.5 Probationary Period

The contractor shall assign employees to the client's premises with the understanding that for the first 90 calendar days that assignment is considered probationary. During this probationary period the client may, at their own discretion, require that the contractor's employee be removed from the contract. On completion of the probationary period, the client will request removal of a contractor employee on a cause basis only.

3.6 On-the-Job Training

Within the probationary period, the contractor shall provide on-the-job training as follows or as specifically appropriate to the substance of services to be delivered.

On-the-job training, as interpreted herein, is only conducted under the supervision of a qualified security officer who has, by practice and experience, a working knowledge of all of the client's systems, procedures, and practices appropriate to the life safety and security matters of the site. The contractor shall provide evidence of the completion of such training, detailing the instruction matters covered and instruction periods in each specific area. The contractor bears the responsibility of coordinating this instruction with the shift supervisor to assure the required protection level is maintained at all times. On-the-job training will be conducted during periods when the trainee is exposed to the maximum learning opportunity as it relates to activity and the ability to participate in active occurrences under the supervision of the senior security officer.

The training will involve the trainee in live performance experience in the areas identified for such time periods as may be deemed reasonable by the instructor for a trainee to learn the complexities of each task. At such time as the assigned training officer advises that the trainee has mastered the requirements of a particular area, a new area of training will be undertaken. In no case shall the on-the-job training requirement be less than stated above, regardless of the entry-level experience of the trainee. The learning emphasis will be as follows:

On-the-Job 1: Prevention/Protection
    Patrol requirements
    Communication system use and procedure
    Use of vehicles
    Hazard identification: initial action and reporting
    Identification systems
    Package screening procedures
    Client/contractor reporting requirements
    Receiving dock operations and procedures
    Response to fire and intrusion alarms and reports
    Responsibilities of individual posts for timely intervention response to
        alarms and emergency situations
    Traffic and parking control and enforcement
    Specific escort requirements
    Appearance, bearing, and demeanor

On-the-Job 2: Enforcement
    Techniques of handling confrontations with:
        Client's employees
        Client's visitors
        Client's contractors

    Techniques of handling normal business contacts with:
        Client's employees
        Client's senior executives
        Client's visitors
        Client's special guests
        Client's contractors

    Specific post instructions
    Enforcement responsibilities of client's procedures and regulations
    Review of criminal law procedures regarding potential site confrontations
    Documentation of and preservation of evidence
    Limitations on search and seizure
    Proper report writing

On-the-Job 3: Emergency Procedures
    Basic first aid practices
    Fire fighting practices
    Evacuation practices
    Bomb search practices
    Power failure practices

On-the-Job 4: Special Equipment Training
    Operation of vehicles

Operation of radio communication systems
Console operation practices
Operation of computerized alarm and access control systems

3.7 Skill Level Categories

The contractor is advised that beyond the status of probationary officer, six distinct levels are recognized as existing in the assignment of contract employees to the client's service. A general description of each skill category is provided below in an ascending skill level from least skilled to most skilled. It is the client's interpretation that probationary security officers must have successfully completed not less than the 12.5 hours of classroom training and the prescribed on-the-job training specified in section 3.6 to be considered qualified to fill the least-skilled category.

Skill Level 1: Probationary Security Officer

This skill level involves the delivery of services on a specific fixed post. The procedures for accountability, observation and inspection, courteous and efficient deportment, and documentation of activities are the essential skills that must be tailored to the post requirement. The posts are not a location or time where continual contact with the public will occur.

Skill Level 2: Security Officer II

This skill level involves a combination of fixed and mobile posts where the opportunity for normal business contact and confrontation experience will be more frequent. On an ascending level of capability, appearance, bearing and demeanor assume more significance because of the increased employee and public contact. A higher degree of technical knowledge is required in reference to the limitations in authority and the enforcement of site regulations and the scope of activities and areas with which the security officer must maintain a working knowledge.

Skill Level 3: Security Officer III

This skill level involves a more complete knowledge of all post requirements and as such represents the essential passage of time necessary to gain the basic knowledge of a variety of posts. The technical skill required is representative of the peak of skill capability both in emergency response requirements, the handling of confrontations, and the successful interface of the protective force with client employees, visitors, and contractors.

Skill Level 4: Security Officer IV

This skill level represents the requirement for a complete operational knowledge of the life/safety and security system and the responsibilities and response capabilities of each post in an active status. Beyond the high degree of technical and procedural knowledge is the requirement to exercise disciplined response decisions in directing security officers to meet the various normal and emergency service requirements that will occur.

Skill Level 5: Sergeant

This skill level requires a complete and thorough knowledge of the life/safety, security, and administrative system appropriate to the secure maintenance of the client's site. A capability must exist to make disciplined response decisions in directing security officers to meet the necessities of developing emergency situations. The individual must be capable of executing command decisions that promote and maintain the best interests of the client at all times. A capability to administer to the demands and necessities of the protective requirements on a given shift, while exercising due regard for individual skill levels and cost-effective staffing assignment, shall be exercised at all times.

Skill Level 6: Lieutenant

This skill level requires tested and proven supervisory capabilities. This person is required to have a working knowledge of all posts for all shifts. They will be required to participate with training, developing, and disciplining subordinates on an assigned shift. This skill level will require a capability to maintain control over performance and costs.

3.8 Performance Evaluation

The contractor shall be responsible for performing, documenting, and making available to the client a performance evaluation of each contract employee, no less than twice annually. The substance of this evaluation will include an appraisal of the following areas:

> Appearance, bearing, and demeanor
> Attitude, reliability, and punctuality
> Technical knowledge of performance requirements
> Procedural knowledge of client requirements
> Leadership capability and potential
> Special areas of competence

3.9 Merit Increases

The client reserves the right to grant merit increases to specific security officers based on the client's opinion and belief of the individual's capabilities and contribution to the client's interests. Any merit increases will not exceed 2% of the current wage rate of the individual security officer and will have no influence on any scheduled wage increases defined in the contract for longevity of service.

3.10 On-site Supervisory Responsibilities

The contractor shall appoint a senior contract security officer who will be respon-sive to the designated Contract Monitor. This officer will be responsible for the control and accuracy of time records for all contract personnel and exercise over-all supervision and direction of the guard force. In addition, they will assist with the selection and screening process of new candidates and will possess security training instructor capabilities. This supervisor will also discipline, replace, and transfer personnel when necessary.

3.11 Temporary Personnel

The client may, from time to time, identify a need for additional, temporary se-curity officers to fulfill a temporary service. As time permits, the client shall attempt to provide the contractor with reasonable and timely notice of such re-quirements. In such instances the contractor and client will evaluate the minimum skill requirements and prescreening practices required based on the available lead time and the nature of the temporary service. The contractor shall maintain for this purpose, a reserve list of security officers capable of filling an additional ten posts on a twenty-four-hour, seven-day-a-week basis. In such situations excep-tions to these specification requirements agreed to by the client shall be made only for the duration of the temporary personnel need as provided by the con-tractor.

3.12 Uniform Requirements

The contractor shall provide and maintain the required uniforms necessary for this contract that will directly represent the image of the client. Badges and other insignia to be worn on the security officers' uniforms will be in accordance with any state law that may apply.

4.0 Description of Service Requirements

This section of the specifications will describe the general nature of service re-quired as appropriate to the Statement of Work at specific locations.

SAMPLE 2:   FORMAT FOR PROPOSAL

Proposals being presented in response to the attached Statement of Work shall be submitted as one original and two copies via U.S. mail, or be hand delivered to:

Client's name and address
Attention: _____
To arrive no later than _____ [time/day/month/year].

Proposals shall be in two distinct and separate parts so that each part may be reviewed separately. The parts are to be titled:

Part I: Management/Technical Proposal
Part II: Financial Proposal

Bidders shall exercise care to limit proposal pages to the minimum necessary to provide a concise response to the Statement of Work. The inclusion of promotional and advertising literature in the Proposal will be considered as superfluous material and is discouraged. The exception to this stipulation is the biographical or résumé information regarding contractor executive personnel and/or management personnel and tables of organizational structure. Bidders are encouraged to be innovative and may submit alternative bids. Alternative bids shall not be considered from any bidder who has failed to submit a proposal for the services specified herein. Bidders shall respond to the specifications on a paragraph-by-paragraph basis stating their compliance or exception to the specifications. If no deviation or exception is indicated, it is understood that the services to be furnished will be in full compliance with the specifications and will be appropriate for the intended purposes.

1. Part I: Management/Technical Proposal

This section shall make no discussion of financial matters but will concentrate on detailed responses to the following items:

a. Contractor's Organization and Management Concepts

The contractor's management plan shall describe its organization, and identify the name and responsibilities of all principal management officers and supervisory personnel. The bidder's plan should also include organizational and functional charts and/or tables reflecting lines of management responsibilities. The bidder shall clearly identify the manner in which all aspects of the quality management of security service performance are to be assured. The bidder shall also define the frequency of inspections of post by shift and the use of operational records. The management plan shall describe the means and methods whereby the contractor will respond to the requirements of the mission as defined in the Statement of Work. Bidders' plans shall also address the management procedures for operational, logistical, and administrative support for all functions, including procedures for an efficient transition program at the onset of the contract and personnel replacement and provision of temporary security officers and for the continuity of quality security personnel and services.

b. Contractor's Inspection System

The contractor's management plan shall establish an inspection system covering all of the services specified in the Statement of Work. The inspection system shall specify areas to be inspected on both scheduled and unscheduled bases and include a method of identifying deficiencies in the quality of services performed before the level of performance deteriorates to an unacceptable level. The bidder's proposal shall describe the nature of documentation associated with the inspection process that will be made available to the client's representative for review.

c. Contractor's Recruiting, Screening, and Selection Procedures

Contractor shall explain in detail their policies relating to recruiting, screening, testing, and selection to ensure that only competent, qualified personnel are assigned to the contract in accordance with the qualification criteria specified in the Statement of Work.

d. Training

The bidders will explain their approach to comply with the preassignment, on-the-job, recurring training and special training as stipulated in the Statement of Work.

e. Quality Assurance Program

Bidders shall describe the Quality Control Programs that shall be applied to the performance of this contract to ensure their commitment to continuous improvement and productivity. This description should also describe the manner in which the contractor's quality assurance program will be advantageous to the client's interests and support the quality assurance programs of the client.

2. Part II: Financial Proposal

The bidders shall use this separate section to describe in sufficient detail all costs related to staff-hour schedules for all skill levels of personnel as described in the Statement of Work. All costs and expenses will be explained to include, but are not limited to, vacation, insurance, taxes, licensing, equipment, benefits, management costs, general and administrative expenses, profit, and all other manner of cost and expense associated with this contract. The bidder's response to the financial portion of the proposal shall be delivered in a sealed envelope together with the Management/Technical Proposal, or as a separate volume to the Proposal. To be responsive, the contractor must propose a firm, fixed-price contract.

3. Closing Date

Bidders' proposals must be received no later than _____ (A.M./P.M.) on [date and year] _____ . Extensions beyond this date will not be granted, nor will modifications to the proposals be accepted beyond this date, unless the client regards such requests for extensions to be in their interest. It is the responsibility of the contractor to ensure that all proposals are received by the client in a timely manner. The anticipated effective date of the contract is 12:01 A.M., [date and year] _____ .

4. Questions and Exceptions

All questions and exceptions regarding the Request for Proposal and Statement of Work and the execution thereof shall be submitted in writing or via electronic facsimile transmission to the client's Contract Monitor. All questions and exceptions must be stated clearly and be accompanied by supporting data when applicable. No telephone inquiries will be accepted. All questions will receive a written response as promptly as possible, but no later than two business days from the time of receipt. If, for any reason, the contractor does not receive the client's response, the client assumes no liability for any inconvenience or loss of capability to the contractor.

5. Type of Contract

It is the client's intent that any contract resulting from this solicitation will be a firm, fixed-price contract. A firm, fixed-price proposal is required to be responsive to the Request for Proposal. Bidders are required to submit proposals, as indicated by the Request for Proposal on all tasks, or none.

6. Use of Subcontractors

The client recognizes the use of subcontractors as an acceptable business practice. If it is anticipated that the contractor will utilize the services of a subcontractor during the term of the contract, the contractor's proposal shall contain explicit data in all sections of the proposal defining which tasks will apply to the contractor and which tasks will apply to the subcontractor. The contractor shall assume total responsibility for all work performed by the subcontractor and shall bear all responsibility for any financial arrangements made between them. The client will not enter into any contractual relationships with the subcontractor. The subcontractor shall be subject to all of the client's rules, regulations, and procedures as are applied to the contractor in the Statement of Work, including the execution of any secrecy agreements for the protection of the client's trade secrets, proprietary information, or other sensitive material.

7. Basis for Contract Award

The proposals of all bidders responding to the Request for Proposal shall be evaluated. Proposals will be evaluated in two phases: the Management and Technical Proposal shall be considered first, and the Financial Proposal will be evaluated last. Each section will be weighed in accordance with the following schedule:

Management Section	_____ points maximum
Technical Capabilities	_____ points maximum
Financial Proposal	_____ points maximum

Proposals shall be ranked in an order ranging from best to least according to the highest points scored as opposed to the lowest. In the rare event of a tie between two bidders, the client shall reserve the right to determine the method by which the successful bidder will be selected. As a result of this evaluation, the client may request additional information or clarification of a questionable issue in either portion. Bidders must respond to these requests in a prompt manner to receive further consideration. The contract will be awarded to that contractor who has demonstrated a clear and comprehensive understanding of the Statement of Work and who, through remarkable qualifications and experience, has proven their professional capabilities to effectively perform the required services to the client's satisfaction in a cost-conscious manner. The client reserves the right to reject any and all proposals.

9. Bidders' Conference and On-site Tour

A bidders' conference will be held on [date and time] _____, at [client's address] _____, and will be immediately followed by a site tour. Bidders are limited to two representatives from each company only. Cameras and tape recorders are prohibited.

10. Designation of Client Representative

The following individual is identified as the sole point of contact for all bidders during this solicitation:

Name _____

Title _____

Address _____

Telephone _____

Fax _____

SAMPLE 3: INVITATION TO BID LETTER

[Buyer's company] _____ invites [Vendor] _____ to submit a proposal to furnish the security services required by the attached Statement of Work at [Buyer's address] _____. Bids shall be on a firm fixed annual price and shall include the cost of furnishing all services, material, and equipment as described in the Statement of Work. The contract shall be for a three year period, with approximately _____ total staff hours, beginning on [date] _____, and terminating on [date] _____.

To qualify as a bidder on this procurement, it will be necessary that your company be represented at a bidders' conference to be held at [Clients address] _____. During the bidders' meeting all questions relating to the Statement of Work and all other questions in reference to this procurement will be answered. Bidders will be limited to no more than two representatives per company. Attendance at this meeting is mandatory for your company to be eligible to bid on this contract.

Bidders are advised to carefully examine the Statement of Work and attached specifications and inform themselves of all conditions and matters that might affect their ability to perform the required services and the cost thereof. In the event a bidder may find discrepancies or omissions in the specifications or any other document associated with this bid, they should bring the matter to our attention at the bidders' conference. Failure to observe or understand all requirements shall not excuse the successful bidder from the responsibility for the complete performance of the Agreement.

This invitation to bid does not commit the Buyer to pay any costs, or to reimburse the bidder for any expenses incurred by the Bidder in the preparation or submission of the proposal, nor should it be construed as a contract or commitment on the part of the Buyer, implicit or otherwise, to accept a bid.

Bids must be accepted at [Buyer's specific department] _____ and [address] _____ no later than [hour] _____, [date] _____, [year] _____. Bids received after this time will not be eligible for further consideration on this solicitation. The buyer retains the right to reject any and all bids.

A successful Bidder will be selected and notified no later than Date _____.

On receipt of this correspondence, the Bidders shall notify [Buyer's contact] _____ at [telephone number] _____ to advise whether your company intends to bid on this procurement.

SAMPLE 4: NONDISCLOSURE AGREEMENT

This Agreement, made and entered into this _____ day of [year] _____ by and between [Vendor] _____, a (corporation/partnership) organized and existing under the laws of the State of _____, having offices located at _____, and [Buyer/Possessor] _____, a corporation organized and existing under the laws of the State of _____, having its principal offices at _____.

Witnesseth

Whereas, the Buyer and Vendor have mutually entered into a legally binding Service Agreement in which the vendor is contractually obligated to provide specifically identified security services to the Buyer; and

Whereas, the Buyer has in its possession certain proprietary information, data, and material that require protection against loss and/or unauthorized disclosure; and

Whereas, the Vendor, agents, employees and assignees may, from time to time, have access to the Buyer's proprietary information in the performance of duties and responsibilities being performed under the conditions of the Service Agreement; and

Whereas, each party desires to protect against unauthorized disclosure or use of any proprietary information disclosed to the Vendor, agents, employees, and assignees in the performance of their duties;

Now therefore, in consideration of the promises and the mutual covenants hereinafter contained, the parties hereby as follows:

1. Definitions

a. "Proprietary Information," for the purposes of this Agreement, is defined as any and all technical data, designs, know-how, trade secrets, drawings, business information (including, but not limited to, sales financial, contractual or marketing information, strategic plans), and other information owned by the possessor that is: (1) designated *Proprietary Information*; (2) in writing, or reduced to writing within thirty days of oral disclosure; and (3) to which the vendor, agents, employees and assigns may either be specifically given or inadvertently have access.

b. Proprietary Information shall not include any information or data that is: (1) Already rightfully in Vendor's possession without breach of this Agreement and without limitation on its disclosure; (2) Independently developed by the Vendor; (3) Publicly disclosed by the Vendor; (4) Rightfully received on a nonproprietary basis by the Vendor from a third party; (5) Approved for release by written agreement with the Buyer; (6) Furnished to a third party without restriction as to use of disclosure; (7) Available by the inspection of products marketed by

Buyer or others; or (8) In the public domain at the time of its receipt or subsequently comes into the public domain through no breach of this Agreement.

2. Disclosure

In connection with the Vendor's undertaking with regard to the Service Agreement, the Buyer may have occasion to disclose to the Vendor information or data deemed to be Proprietary Information. In the event of any such disclosure, the Buyer grants to the Vendor (not including subsidiaries, affiliates, other divisions, or employees who do not have a need to know such information) the right to have access to the Proprietary Information only in connection with work specifically relating to the Service Agreement.

3. Points of Contact

Each party shall designate in writing one or more of its personnel as its exclusive points of contact with respect to resolving any conflicts or questions with respect to this agreement. Each party may change its designated points of contact at any time by written notice to the other party

4. Standards of Care

The Vendor and its agents, employees, and assignees agrees to treat any Proprietary Information it received from the Buyer with the same degree of care and protection that it uses in handling its own information of a similar nature that it does not wish disclosed to others.

5. Exceptions

Nothing herein shall restrict the Vendor from disclosing to others any portion of Proprietary Information:

    a.   Pursuant to a judicial or lawful order, but only to the extent of any
         such order and after notice to the Buyer who may attempt by lawful
         process to prevent such disclosure; or
    b.   If such disclosure occurs despite the exercise of the degree of care
         provided for in Article 4 above.

6. Use of Restrictive Legends

The parties agree that, in the event any documentation or information supplied to the Vendor under this Agreement bears the Buyer's restrictive or proprietary legends, such legends shall not impose any liability or obligation on the Vendor other than as set forth in this Agreement. All such information supplied to the Vendor by the Buyer shall be governed solely by the terms and conditions of this Agreement.

7. Return of Proprietary Information

After the expiration or sooner termination of this Agreement as provided herein, all Proprietary Information released by the Buyer to the Vendor shall be destroyed or returned to the Buyer or be destroyed at the direction of the Buyer, and the Vendor shall have no further right to use, disseminate, or disclose such Proprietary Information except as shall be mutually agreed thereafter.

8. Remedies

Each party agrees that remedies at law may be inadequate to protect against breach of this Agreement. Therefore, Vendor hereby consents to the granting of injunctive relief, whether temporary, preliminary, or final, in favor of the Buyer without proof of actual damages. The remedy does not waive any other action or remedy the Buyer may have at law or in equity.

9. Entire Agreement

This Agreement represents the entire Agreement between the parties with respect to the subject matter hereof and supersedes in its entirety all prior agreements between the parties with respect hereto. No alteration, modification, interpretation, or amendment of this Agreement shall be binding on the parties unless in writing, designated as an amendment hereto and executed with equal formality by each party.

10. Termination

This Agreement becomes effective as of the day and year first above written, and shall remain in force and effect until the first to occur of the following events:

    a.   Mutual consent of the parties evidenced by execution of the recession agreement;

    b.   Substantial default of a party hereto; or

    c.   Expiration of _____ years from the day and year first above written.

In Witness Whereof, each of the parties hereto has caused this Agreement to be executed in its behalf by its duly authorized officer or representative as of the day and year first above written.

SAMPLE 5: BIDDER QUALIFICATIONS QUESTIONNAIRE FOR SECURITY OFFICER SERVICES

A. List five largest accounts under local management

    Name of Account   *Contact Name*   *Telephone*

1. _____
2. _____
3. _____
4. _____
5. _____

B. How many hours of formal preassignment training are provided to guard personnel?

C. How many full-time security officers are assigned to local jurisdiction?

D. What free benefits are offered to full-time security officers?

    1. Vacation
    2. Holiday pay
    3. Hospitalization
    4. Life insurance
    5. Other

E. Can the vendor do business with 6% over cost?   Yes   No

F. Furnish the following payroll tax information

    1. FICA
    2. SUI
    3. FUI
    4. W/C
    5. G/L
    6. Total

G. The vendor has licensed offices in the following states:

    1. _____
    2. _____
    3. _____
    4. _____
    5. _____
    6. _____
    7. _____
    8. _____

H. Is the vendor willing to bid and manage accounts in those States?

    Yes   No

I. Is the vendor prepared to offer armed guards if necessary?   Yes   No

    Exceptions: _____

J. In the vendor's bid, is the vendor willing to break down quoted rates by actual cost, variable and fixed expenses, and profit?   Yes   No

K. What is the vendor's average rate and average wage?

    Rate: $ _____
    Wage: $ _____

L. Attach a copy of vendor's organizational chart, including office staff.

M. Attach a copy of vendor's management staff curricula vitae.

N. Do field supervisors have patrol vehicles equipped with two-way radio or cellular phone?

O. Can they be reached 24 hours each day?   Yes   No

P. Does the vendor have a formal training program for field supervisors?

    Define: _____

Q. How many accounts has the vendor lost during the last calendar year?

    _____

R. Identify two of the largest losses:

    Account Name   *Hours per week*   *Client Contact and Telephone Number*

1. _____
2. _____

S. Does the vendor operate a formal field inspection policy?   Yes   No

    Explain _____

T. Does the vendor have a formal quality assurance program?   Yes   No

    Explain _____

U. Does the vendor have experience in converting proprietary guard forces to a contract security service?   Yes   No

    Specify clients: _____

V. Can the vendor provide investigative services as required?   Yes   No

W. Does the vendor have experience in working with bargaining unit security services?   Yes   No

X. Is the vendor a field office of a national/international security service organization?   Yes   No

If yes, identify home office, location, and provide an organizational chart showing local vendor's relation to its parent organization.

Y. Describe other major protective services provided by local office or parent organization.

1. _____
2. _____
3. _____
4. _____
5. _____

SAMPLE 6: BACKGROUND INVESTIGATION AUTHORIZATION

I, _____, hereby authorize [Requestor] _____ and its agents to conduct an investigation of my personal background, references, character, past employment, education, criminal or police records, medical records, credit information, including those maintained by private and public organizations and institutions, and all other public records necessary for the purpose of confirming the information contained on my application for employment and/or obtaining other information that may be relevant to my qualifications for employment or any other issue pertinent to it.

I release [Requestor] _____ and/or its agents, representatives, and any other person or entity either public or private, which provides information pursuant to this authorization, from any and all liabilities, claims, libel, or any other nature of litigation whether at law or in equity with regard to the information obtained from any and all of the above sources mentioned.

The following is my true and complete legal name and all information provided hereinafter is true and correct to the best of my knowledge and belief.

Name _____

Birth Name and Other Names Used _____

Present Address _____

City and State _____ Zip Code _____

Former Address _____ Zip Code _____

Date of Birth _____ Social Security No. _____

Driver's License No. _____ Issuing State _____

Signature_____ Date _____

SAMPLE 7: PROFESSIONAL CONSULTING SERVICES AGREEMENT

This Agreement, made on _____ between an individual, _____, hereinafter referred to as the "Consultant" and _____ hereafter referred to as "Client."

Whereas Client and Consultant desire to enter into an agreement for the performance by Consultant of professional services in connection with activities of Client. In consideration of the premises and of the mutual promises herein, the parties hereto agree as follows:

The Consultant agrees to provide to Client the consulting services as specified in Exhibit A in accordance with the terms and conditions contained in this Agreement.

1. Term

The consultant shall coordinate its work efforts and maintain a liaison with the Client Monitor named in Exhibit A, or with a duly appointed representative. Unless terminated in accordance with provisions of Article 9 hereof, these services shall be performed during the period shown in Exhibit A, or up to the completion of the project as defined in Exhibit A.

2. Payment for Services Rendered

For providing services as defined herein, Client shall pay the Consultant the amount and according to the schedule specified in Exhibit A.

In no event shall Client be obligated to pay Consultant for its services and travel and related expenses in excess of the authorized Ceiling Dollar Amount specified in Exhibit A.

3. Consultant's Warranties

The Consultant hereby warrants that no other party has exclusive rights to its services in the specific areas described herein and that Consultant is in no way compromising any rights or trust relationships between any other party and Consultant, or creating a conflict of interest, or any possibility thereof, for Consultant and Client. The Consultant further warrants that all services provided hereunder will be performed in accordance with all applicable federal, state, or local laws and executive orders. Consultant agrees to indemnify and hold Client harmless from any and all claims of other parties for breach of these warranties.

4. Indemnity and Insurance

The Consultant shall indemnify and hold Client harmless from any liability for injury or damage caused by the Consultant to persons or property during the performance of the Agreement. Neither the existence of nor the assent of Client to the types of limits of insurance carried by the Consultant shall be deemed a waiver or release of the Consultant's liability of responsibility under this Agreement. Consultant shall carry the following minimal insurance coverage in a form acceptable to Client during the term of this Agreement: Comprehensive Automobile Liability Insurance with coverage limits of $500,000 per occurrence for any and all injury, death, or property damage.

5. Nature of Relationship

Consultant herein is an independent contractor and will not act as an agent for the Client nor shall be deemed an employee of Client for purposes of any employment benefit program or be deemed an employee of Client for purposes of income tax withholding, F.I.C.A. taxes, unemployment benefits, or otherwise. The Consultant shall not enter into any agreement or incur any obligations on Client's behalf, or commit Client in any manner without Client's prior written consent. As an independent contractor, the Consultant understands and agrees that it is solely responsible for the control and supervision of the means by which the project defined in Exhibit A is completed. Such means, by which the project is accomplished, are subject to Consultant's discretion, which discretion must be exercised consistent with the goal of completing the project on schedule and in accordance with the terms of this Agreement. The Consultant also agrees and understands that no training is required for the performance of this project, nor will any training be provided by the Client. Any supplies, which in the option of the Consultant, may be necessary to perform the services required, shall be the responsibility of the Consultant.

6. Inventions, Patents, Copyright, and Technology

Consultant shall promptly and fully disclose to Client any and all inventions, works of authorship and mask works, including all improvement, discoveries, ideas, technologies, know-how, work products, concepts, material, disclosures, software programs, computer language, programming aids, documentation, or any other intellectual property, conceived, developed, originated, fixed, or reduced to practice by Consultant and/or its employees in connection with, or as a result of, consulting services performed for Client and shall treat all such information as if it were proprietary information furnished to Consultant by Client.

   Consultant agrees to assign, and does hereby assign to Client, for the consideration paid under this Agreement, the entire right, title and interest, or such lesser interest as Client may in any particular case choose to accept, in and to each and all of the inventions, works of authorship and mask works set forth above whether or not patentable or copyrightable. Consultant further agrees to execute, and cause its employees to execute, all applications for patents and/or copyrights, domestic and foreign, assignments and other papers necessary to secure and enforce rights related to any and all of the inventions, works of authorship and mask works. If Consultant and/or its employees are needed at any time to give testimony for Client, in any proceeding affecting patents and/or copyrights described above, Consultant shall do so and cause its employees to do so and Consultant shall be paid at the rate set forth in Exhibit A (if this Agreement is in force) or at a rate to be mutually agreed (if this Agreement has been terminated), plus reasonable expenses.

7. Safeguarding Client's Trade Secrets and Data

Consultant agrees that it shall not divulge to anyone either during the term of this Agreement or thereafter any of Client's trade secrets or other proprietary data or information of any kind whatsoever acquired by Consultant in carrying out the terms of this Agreement.

Consultant further agrees that on completion or termination of this Agreement, it will turn over to Client or make such disposition thereof as may be directed or approved by Client, any notebook, data, information, or other material acquired or compiled by Consultant in carrying out the terms of this Agreement.

8. Miscellaneous

a. Waivers

No failure on the part of either party to exercise, and no delay in exercising, any right or remedy hereunder shall operate as a waiver thereof; nor shall any single or partial exercise of any right or remedy hereunder preclude any other of further exercise thereof or the exercise of any other right or remedy granted hereby or by any related document or by law.

b. Governing Law

This Agreement shall be deemed to be a contract made under the laws of _____ and for all purposes it, plus any related or supplemental documents and notices, shall be construed in accordance with and governed by the law of such state.

c. Amendments

This Agreement may not be and shall not be deemed or construed to have been modified, amended, rescinded, canceled, or waived in whole or in part, except by written instruments signed by the parties hereto.

d. Entire Agreement

This Agreement, including Exhibit A attached hereto and made a part hereof, constitutes and expresses the entire agreement and understanding between the parties. All previous discussions, promises, representation, and understandings between the parties relative to this Agreement, if any, have been merged into this document.

9. Termination

Without limiting any rights the Client may have for reason of any default by Consultant, Client reserves the right to terminate this Agreement in whole or in part at its convenience by written notice. Such termination shall be effective in the manner and on the date specified in said notice and shall be without prejudice to any claims the Client may have against the Consultant. Aside from any continuing work, Client's sole obligation in the event of such termination shall be to reimburse Consultant for services actually performed by Consultant up to the effective date of such termination.

Termination shall not relieve Consultant of its continuing obligations under this Agreement, particularly the requirements of Articles 6 and 7 above.

10. Invoicing and Payment

Consultant shall submit invoices to the Client Monitor based on the payment schedule in Exhibit A. Invoices shall reference this Agreement Number and the time period of authorized performance involved and shall have attached hereto receipts for all travel expenses claimed by Consultant.

Provided that such travel is authorized in Exhibit A, client will reimburse Consultant for reasonable travel and related expenses incurred by Consultant away from its home base in connection with the services defined in Exhibit A.

Invoices submitted by the Consultant must be approved by the Client Monitor or his/her appointed representative.

11. Client Security and Safety Requirements

The Consultant will inform all of its employees engaged in work under this Agreement and instruct them to honor the Client confidentiality requirements set forth in Article 7 of this Agreement and/or any security and safety requirements appended to this Agreement. Failure of an employee to honor such requirements will be considered a material breach leading to (i) removal of the employee as a contracted worker under this Agreement, and (ii) if the gravity of the violation warrants, at client's own discretion, termination of this Agreement for default.

12. Dispute Resolution

a. Notification

Before bringing any action or other proceeding ("action"), Consultant will promptly notify client at its address for written communications (shown on page one of this Agreement) of any dispute it has with client under this Agreement.

b. Management Review Process

No "action" will be brought by Consultant against client until: (1) senior management of both parties conducts a study of the dispute or disagreement; (2) a meeting between the parties is held to try to resolve the dispute; and (3) if after such meeting takes place, one of the parties sends a letter to the other stating it is unable to resolve the matter in dispute.

13. Conflict of Interest

Consultant agrees that it will not, while performing under this Agreement create a conflict of interest that may prove to be detrimental to the interest of Client. The responsibility to notify client of any potential conflict of interest rests with the Consultant. Client agrees to promptly evaluate and notify Consultant of its decision.

14. Subcontracting and Assignments

It is understood and agreed that this Agreement is for the rendering of consulting services by Consultant who is acting as an independent contractor. Consultant may not subcontract any part or all of the services to be provided without written consent of client; however, Consultant may, at its own expense, use assistance to accomplish the services required by this Agreement.

15. Disclosure

Consultant acknowledges and agrees that it may be necessary for client to disclose the fact of the Consultant's retention, the duties performed, and the compensation paid, should there be proper inquiry from such a source as an authorized U.S. governmental agency or should client believe it has a legal obligation to disclose such information and Consultant hereby authorizes any such disclosures.

CONSULTANT: CLIENT:

_____   _____

DATE: DATE:

_____   _____

Agreement for Consulting Services

Exhibit A

    Agreement No. _____

    Consultant Name: _____

    Client Monitor:_____

    Address: _____

Term of Agreement

    I.   Services to be rendered
        Consultant to provide the following services:

    II. Compensation and payment schedule
            A. Compensation for consulting services
            B. Travel and related expenses

    III. Ceiling dollar amount

SAMPLE 8: CONFLICT OF INTEREST STATEMENT

The undersigned warrants that, to the best of the undersigned Consultant's knowledge and belief, and in addition to any information that has been otherwise disclosed, there are no relevant facts or information that could be construed as a conflict of interest to the client and that the undersigned Consultant has disclosed all relevant information.

The undersigned agrees that if such a conflict of interest becomes known, it is the Consultant's responsibility to make an immediate and complete disclosure of such fact in writing to the Client and shall include a description of the action taken, or will take to avoid or mitigate such conflicts.

Consultant _____ Date _____

Bibliography

The following sources have provided information, thoughts, concepts, and ideas to this book.

Axelrod, Alan. *The War Between the Spies: A History of Espionage during the American Civil War.* New York: Atlantic Press, 1952.

Beer, Stafford. *Platform for Change.* New York: John Wiley and Sons, 1975.

Bennis, W. G. *Changing Organizations.* New York: McGraw-Hill, 1966.

Bowman, Joel P., and Bernadine P. Branschaw. *How to Write Proposals That Produce.* Phoenix, AZ: Oryx Press, 1992.

Brown, George William. *Baltimore and the 19th of April 1861.* Baltimore, MD: Johns Hopkins University, 1887.

Canton, Lucien G. *Guard Force Management.* Boston: Butterworth–Heinemann, 1996.

Champy, James. *Reengineering Management.* New York: HarperCollins, 1995.

Collins, Patrick. *Living in Troubled Lands.* Boulder, CO: Paladin Press, 1981.

Cook, Desmond. *Program Evaluation and Review Techniques.* Washington, DC: Superintendent of Documents, 1971.

Commandant, USAMPS. *Physical Security: FM 19-30.* Ft. McClellan, AL, 1971.

"Culturgrams." Provo, UT: David M. Kennedy Center for International Studies, Brigham Young University, 1986.

Dalton, Dennis. *Security Management: Business Strategies for Success.* Boston: Butterworth–Heinemann, 1995.

———. *The Art of Successful Security Management.* Boston: Butterworth–Heinemann, 1998.

Davis, Curtis Carroll. "The Civil War's Most Over-rated Spy." *West Virginia History* (October 1968).

Drucker, Peter. *Management: Tasks, Responsibilities, Practices.* New York: Harper and Row, 1954.

———. *The Practice of Management.* New York: Harper and Row, 1954.

Felton, C. C. "The Baltimore Plot." *Harvard Monthly* (December 1885).

Forrester, Jay W. *Industrial Dynamics.* Cambridge, MA: MIT Press, 1961.

Hammer, Michael, and Steven A. Stanton. *The Reengineering Revolution.* New York: HarperCollins, 1995.

Harne, Eric G. "Partnering with Security Providers." *Security Management* (March 1998).

Holtz, Herman. *How to Succeed as an Independent Consultant.* New York: John Wiley and Sons, 1993.

———. *Consultant's Guide to Proposal Writing.* New York: John Wiley and Sons, 1986.

Horan, James D. *The Pinkertons: The Detective Dynasty That Made History.* New York: Bonanza Books, 1967.

Horowitz, Sherry L. "Security's Positive Return." *Security Management* (October 1997).

Janes, Timothy T. "Keeping Control of Contracts." *Security Management* (July 1995).

Johnson, Dennis L. "A Team Approach to Threat Assessment." *Security Management* (September 1994).

Kantor, Rosabeth. *The Challenge of Organizational Change.* New York: Harper and Row, 1984.

Kobetz, Richard W., ed. *Providing Executive Protection.* Berryville, VA: Executive Protection Institute. 1991.

Koontz, Harold, and Cyril O'Donnell. *Principles of Management.* New York: McGraw-Hill, 1972.

Laman, Ward Hill. *Recollections of Abraham Lincoln.* Washington DC: Tilliard, 1895.

Ledoux, Darryl T. "Exploding the Myths of Contract Security." *Security Management* (January 1995).

Mancuso, Joseph R. *How to Write a Winning Business Plan.* New York: Prentice-Hall, 1985.

March, James G., and Herbert A. Simon. *Organizations.* New York: Wiley Publications, 1958.

Marquet, Chris. "Stranger in a Strange Land." *Security Management* (June 1996).

McKee, Bradford. "Turn Your Workers into a Team." *Nations Business* (July 1992).

Mogelever, Jacob. *Death to Traitors: The Story of General Lafayette C. Baker, The Forgotten Secret Service of Abraham Lincoln.* New York: Doubleday, 1960.

Morn, Frank. *The Eye That Never Sleeps: A History of the Pinkerton Detective Agency.* Bloomington: Indiana University Press, 1982.

Nelson, Raleigh. *Writing the Technical Report.* New York: McGraw-Hill, 1940.

Pearson, Robert. "Weighing and Measuring Security Performance Through the Use of an Audit." *Security Technology and Design* 6 (November 1995).

Peters, Tom. *Liberation Management.* New York: Alfred A. Knopf, 1992.

———. *Thriving on Chaos.* New York: Alfred A. Knopf, 1988.

Post, Richard S. *Determining Security Needs.* Madison, WI: Oak Security Publications, 1973.

Roberts, Richard D. "Vulnerability Analysis: Building Bench Strength with the Corporate Team." *Security Technology and Design* 7 (March 1997).

———. "Changing of the Guard: Corporate Downsizing's Effect on Security." *Security Design and Technology* 6 (October 1996).

Ross, Gerald, and Michael Kay. *Toppling the Pyramids.* New York: Times Books, 1994.

Roughton, James E. "When Contractors Fall Short." *Security Management* (March 1996).

Schaub, James L., and Ken D. Biery. *The Ultimate Security Survey.* Boston: Butterworth–Heinemann, 1994.

Senate Committee on Education and Labor. *Investigations in Relation to the Employment for Private Purposes of Armed Bodies of Men or Detectives in Connection with Differences Between Workmen and Employers.* 52nd Cong., 2d sess., 1893, S. Rpt. 1280.

Sennewald, Charles A. *Security Consulting.* Boston: Butterworth–Heinemann, 1989.

Smith, Geoffey L., Director, General Services, The Arbitron Corp., Columbia, MD, personal interview.

Tarkington, Fran, and Tad Tuleja. *How to Motivate People: The Team Strategy for Success.* New York: Harper and Row, 1986.

Tichy, Noel. *Managing Strategic Change.* New York: John Wiley and Sons, 1983.

Trent, Alexander B. *Guard Contract Kit: A Guide to Cost Effective Security Guard Contract Negotiations.* Fredricksville, OH: ATA, 1993.

———. *Security Survey: A Guide to Analysis of Criticality and Vulnerability Factors of Security Programs.* Colorado Springs, CO: ATA, 1991.

U.S. Department of State. *Background Notes.* Washington, DC: United States Government Printing Office, 1995.

———. *Terrorist Tactics and Security Practices Office of Intelligence and Threat Analysis.* Washington, DC: Bureau of Diplomatic Security, 1994.

———. *Personal Security Guidelines for the American Business Traveler Overseas.* Washington, DC: Overseas Security Advisory Council, 1994.

Urwick, Lydall F., ed. *The Golden Book of Management.* London: Newman Neame, 1956.

Walla, J. Robert. "Contracting with Confidence." *Security Management* (February 1996).

Walsh, Timothy, and Richard J. Healy. *Protection of Assets Manual.* Santa Monica, CA: Merritt, 1991.

Wayne, Curtis B. "Blueprint for Security." *Security Management* (June 1995).

Woodward, Joan. *Industrial Organization: Theory and Practice.* New York: Oxford University Press, 1965.

Index